Shout 85258 is a free, confidential, 24/7 text messaging support service for anyone who is struggling to cope. Our trained volunteers are there round the clock to listen to you and help you take your next steps towards feeling better. Every day we have conversations with children, young people and adults who are facing issues such as suicidal thoughts, depression, anxiety, loneliness, relationships, self-harm and abuse.

Text SHOUT to 85258 to start a conversation at any time of day or night.
Support is only a text away.

Visit giveusashout.org

100 THINGS I LOVE ABOUT CAMBRIDGE UNITED

Supported by Cambridge United Football Club

Written & edited by
Russell Greaves

Layout & cover design by
David Marshall

Photographs by
Simon Lankester, Ben Phillips & Gordon Theobald

Proofreading by
Peter Hanson

Published by
Biddles

British Library Cataloguing in Publication Data.
A catalogue record for this book is available from the British Library.

ISBN 978-1-914408-75-5

About the author

Russell Greaves was born in Cambridge in 1985 and attended his first United match in 2000, a 2-1 loss to Barnet in the Auto Windscreens Shield providing an instructive introduction to life as a U's fan.

A sports journalist with over a decade of experience in the industry, Russell has covered a host of major events, including the Olympic Games, the FIFA World Cup and the Ryder Cup, but has graced no sporting arena that has thrilled him more than a trip to the Abbey.

He also devised, co-wrote and edited the book Cambridge United: 100 Years, 50 Memorable Matches, excerpts from which appear in this work.

Russell lives in East Yorkshire with his wife Leanne and daughter Amelie.

You can find Russell on Twitter (@russgreaves).

Author's note

Like any good book, it was the title for this one that came first. What came next was the startling realisation that one hundred is a rather large number. After sitting alone with that bothersome thought and compiling a list that fell some way short of triple figures, I knew I needed to take a different approach; I had to get some help.

Fortunately, it was not in short supply and to that end I am indebted to the many people I spoke to for this book, whether they are quoted on the following pages or not. It was a continual source of amazement to me that I could approach someone out of the blue – someone who presumably had better things to do than speak to me – and they would be so readily available to talk, in many cases at great length, about Cambridge United.

By the time of completing the final interview, one hundred suddenly seemed like a very small number. Alas, 126 Things I Love About Cambridge United did not have the same ring to it; a line has to be drawn somewhere.

I must give special thanks to a number of people without whom this project would not have been possible. I will list them here and offer my deepest thanks, but you all deserve more words of praise than would fit this page. Thank you to David Marshall, Gareth Daniels, Godric Smith, Will Hunting-Jones, Doug Shulman, Josh Coulson, Harrison Dunk, Paul Wanless, Vic Akers, Ben Phillips, Simon Lankester, Victoria Hornby, Dave Matthew-Jones, Oli Kane and Leanne Greaves.

My gratitude also extends to everyone who has purchased this book. I hope you enjoy this journey through just a small selection of the many things there are to love about this great football club of ours.

Up the U's!

For Leanne & Amelie

x

Foreword
Nick Hornby

Between 1976 and 1984, the Abbey Stadium was my happy place. Those old enough to remember will know that the conventional route to football happiness was not available in the last year of that era: Cambridge United set a new Football League record for most successive games without a win, but it didn't stop me from going; indeed, once it became clear that something extraordinary was happening, you couldn't have kept me away. But in those first few years, the team brought a much more uncomplicated joy. The first year I watched them, Ron Atkinson led them to the Fourth Division championship; the second year, John Docherty, the Doc, took them to the extraordinary heights of the Second Division and games against West Ham, Newcastle, Leicester, Fulham and Crystal Palace.

The Abbey and Cambridge United had everything you needed to feed a serious football addiction. It was walking distance from where I lived, first as a student and then as a teacher in a town centre comprehensive school; it was cheap (although all football was cheap back then); it had a terrific atmosphere; it had a long covered side along one side of the ground, the Habbin Stand, which offered an elevated view from the halfway line and the opportunity to shift from one end to the other at half-time; an excellent sweet shop on the walk to the stadium (Jack Reynolds, the Rock King); the away fans were forced to stand on an open terrace called the Allotments End; and, after a win, 'I've Got A Lovely Bunch Of Coconuts' was played over the tannoy. Perhaps a club historian knows why, but my friends and I didn't, and the sheer randomness and inappropriateness never failed to bring joy.

And I loved the players, because they were lovable. I have watched football regularly ever since, mostly at Highbury and the Emirates, and I have rarely seen a side with so much character. Alan Biley, the deadly, whippety striker who went on to play for Derby and Everton. And Lindsay 'Wolfie' Smith, who just played a lot of games for Cambridge, mostly as a defender, although he could make a sudden and unexpected attacking charge from unexpected areas of the pitch; Brendon Batson, one of Arsenal's first black players, who seemed in retrospect to be taking a rest in the Fourth Division before playing in the First with Ron Atkinson's brilliant West Brom team. Steve Fallon was Tony Adams before Tony Adams had been invented; Tom Finney wasn't the Tom Finney you may have heard of, the one who played for England in the 1950s, but he could have been – he had the same throwback lived-in face and a post-war disregard for his own safety. Steve Spriggs was small and everywhere, and had a terrific shot on him. Later, when Cambridge got really bad, we watched a teenage Andy Sinton and an only slightly older David Moyes, both of whom played throughout the hilariously grisly losing streak. I wish they all played within walking distance of my house now.

The losing streak ended on 11th April, 1984. Cambridge were already relegated; the visitors, Newcastle United, were looking for promotion. Up front for Newcastle were Peter Beardsley, Kevin Keegan and Chris Waddle. In theory, both teams were in the same division; in practice, we were watching England versus San Marino. Cambridge won 1-0, hanging on to their slender lead for what seemed like several weeks, and the joy of the home fans – who by this time were so few in number that we had been forced onto two sides of the ground to make room for the thousands and thousands of visiting fans – was expressed with both volume and disbelief.

I have seen my 'main' team, Arsenal, win countless trophies since. I have seen them go an entire season unbeaten, in a mirror image of Cambridge's 1983-84 season; I have seen them win the league with a last-minute goal, I have seen Bergkamp, Henry, Pires and Vieira do unbelievable things in front of me week after week. But that win over Newcastle was, in the three or four minutes after the final whistle, every bit as elating. Here's what football pleasure is: you beat your head against the wall, over and over again, and every now and again, you stop. Sometimes you stop for a season, or even a decade, or just for five minutes, it doesn't matter. It all comes down to the same thing. Sooner or later you have to start up again. That 83-84 season, Cambridge fans beat their head against the wall in double time, and so the relief was even sweeter. Enjoy your season, and take the respite wherever you can find it.

1. A mentally healthy club
Godric Smith

To be a Cambridge United supporter. The highs, the lows. The moments of pure joy. The inevitable defeats that can transform your mood in an instant – and which thankfully are soon forgotten. We feel it all. The roller coaster ride of the past few decades at United has been more white-knuckle than most, but all we can do is give the team and club our support.

And support matters more now than ever for everyone amid the coronavirus pandemic, which is why the work the club does on mental health has come to the fore as we have all dealt with the fragility of our own mental health during this once-in-a-generation event. Some have had it particularly hard – and a big shout out to U's fan Connor O'Reilly for talking so bravely, eloquently and publicly about his struggles, as detailed in this book. You are not alone.

Among the many reasons to love this club is the work it has done in the community – hat tip to Jez George for having the vision to set up the Trust all those years ago – and the prioritisation of mental health support, with schemes such as Mind Your Head and drop-in sessions that are held at the club with the NHS to help reach people who might be reluctant to go along to their doctor, as well as a dedicated Mental Health Officer as part of the Cambridge United Supporters Panel so fans know they have someone to talk to. It all underpins the club's ambition to have mental health in our DNA, to be a 'mentally healthy club'.

This is an area where our leadership in football has been recognised nationally and where we are playing our own part in shifting the dial from a deep-rooted culture of 'keep quiet and carry on' to one where it is okay to say that you are not okay.

This club has been a huge positive for my mental health in good times and bad. The stories recounted on these pages underline the joy that a football club like ours can bring to supporters. Support makes us all stronger. Support each other and know that if you need help you can reach out as Cambridge United genuinely wants to be Here for U's.

2. Chris Turner
Mark Saggers

When I was presenting on Radio Cambridgeshire in the 1980s, Chris Turner came to Cambridge as manager. I rang him up and told him I wanted to come and watch the team train and he was okay with that, so along I went. I spent the next four years training with Cambridge every day, I became a sort of player liaison officer, I even played for the reserve team now and again.

Chris told me that as long as I didn't share any inside information on the radio, we would get along fine. He kept his side of the bargain, I kept mine, and we developed a wonderful relationship. Chris and his wife Lynne became like my mum and dad. Chris and John Beck were ushers at my wedding.

As a coach he was very hands-on; he worked his players hard but he looked after all of them and they became part of his family. He was someone who knew how to be a leader but he always did things in the right way and he earned the respect and admiration of his players. Chris had this ability to make everybody feel good and when you've got a team that wants to play for the boss, rather than just a bunch of individuals in it for themselves, it works every time.

He was very good at recognising other people's strengths and knowing when to let them get on with their job. He did that with the likes of Becky and Gary Johnson. More than anything, Chris wanted his players and staff to succeed – I don't think that's a given for all managers, but with Chris there was a genuine desire to see others fulfil their potential.

I used to keep him company when he would go to scout players. He wanted to look at Laurie Ryan, who was a prolific scorer in non-League. Chris always wanted to see them play away from home but he would never go and sit in the box like the other scouts; we would go in disguise. That's just the sort of thing he did.

Chris was the man who spotted a lot of the great talent that made up the team which Becky took to the brink of the Premier League. You have to remember the situation the club was in when Chris arrived – they had to apply for re-election the previous season. Without Chris Turner, it's possible the club wouldn't even be here now. He was Cambridge United's man for all seasons.

3. Coming back from the brink
Nick Pomery

We had no idea about the political minefield we were stumbling into. With the Inland Revenue and the Football Association at loggerheads over the payment of creditors, the impasse had already led to Hornchuch going under. The next club to go into administration was Cambridge United.

When this all blew up, it struck me that there wasn't really anyone else who could step into the situation but me – it needed an accountant, someone with the right background, enough time to commit to it, and the will to do it. There was one moment that really gave me the impetus, which came at the game when relegation was confirmed against Rochdale. I was walking out after the game and an old lady in her seventies reached over the barrier and said to me: 'I'm really grateful for what you're doing, I'm just so glad my husband died last year so that he didn't have to see this' – that broke me. I knew then I had to give it my best shot.

The club owed around £850,000 and this was after the ground had been sold. Our largest creditor by some way was the Inland Revenue, meaning they were controlling creditors – they had the final say on any settlement; if they said no, that would effectively bankrupt the club. The Inland Revenue had a bee in their bonnet about being removed as preferred creditors and it was their view if they did not have that privilege, then nobody else should. However, the FA's rule was that football creditors should be paid first and this was a cause of huge tension between them; it had become quite personal.

We had a trump card in Godric Smith, who understood the political machinations. He urged us to get people writing in to raise the issue – in that year, Parliament received more letters on this issue than any other. We gave the Minister for Sport, Richard Caborn, legal justification to get involved and that significantly strengthened our hand to negotiate.

We were summoned to a meeting with the Inland Revenue and the FA. The clock was ticking and the club was perilously close to the brink. Caborn said to the Inland Revenue: 'I really hope you're not going to say no to me.' You could see them quite discomfited as they were forced to relent, on the condition they would have further talks with the FA over the Football Creditors Rule. 'Well,' Caborn said to the FA, 'that seems quite reasonable.' And they too wilted – we had an agreement.

4. The floodlights

The four floodlights that stand proudly in each corner of the Abbey Stadium first took up their watch in 1964 and have towered over the hallowed turf ever since, each steel pylon bearing inscrutable witness to the club's many highs and lows from an unmatched vantage point.

At eighty feet high, the colossal structures are most impressive when each of the twenty-four bulbs that adorn them are burning bright, bathing the pitch in a warm glow. When lit, they can be seen from far across the city and never fail to draw admiring glances from fans making their way over Barnwell Bridge.

There is something undeniably special about a game under the lights at the Abbey, but the enduring presence of that quartet of imposing overseers should not be taken for granted. Back in the 1980s it was found the floodlights were overloaded and posed a safety risk in high winds.

Acting quickly to address the problem, United became one of the first clubs to install the Philips ArenaVision lighting system, taking the lux levels from three hundred to one thousand – a standard required for the Premier League. However, it is said the first time the new lights were turned on, it dimmed half of Ditton Fields as the power usage was so high.

They are now turned on in installments, with thirty seconds between each switch being flicked, while it takes around eight minutes for all four to shine at their brilliant best, which is around seven hundred lux these days. It costs approximately £300 a time to run the floodlights, based on them stirring into life at 6.30 p.m. and remaining lit for four hours or so. As for the bulbs, they cost in the region of £250 each but mercifully they last for up to ten years.

Ahead of the 2021-22 season, contractors were brought in to spruce up the floodlights, abseiling down to fix nuts and bolts and apply fresh paint. It's not a task you'd catch stadium manager and head groundsman Ian Darler carrying out as, by his own admission, he "does not like even going up steps."

5. The Academy
Tom Pell

I've been at the club fifteen years, working my way up to being Academy manager, and in that time the set-up has changed beyond recognition. The club had scrapped the youth scheme and it was restarted by Jez George, Steve Lilley and myself back in 2006.

We were starting from scratch but we had this legacy of negativity over how the old set-up had been disbanded, so we were trying to build relationships again and get the right people in and it was pretty tough. Being outside the League, we didn't have any funding or protection for our players, so in the early days we were constantly losing our best prospects.

Everything changed when that final whistle went at Wembley in 2014 – it was the most unbelievable feeling. Firstly, just as a fan it was a cause for celebration, but crucially it meant we were now a fully-fledged, licensed Academy within the EPPP system, meaning we got funding and compensation if our players went elsewhere. After eight years without any of that, it meant a lot. There are players who started with us in those early days before promotion who have come through and featured in the first team, with Luke Berry probably the most notable – but Leon Davies and Ben Worman are two others who have done the same, while others have gone elsewhere, like Jackson Ramm.

Our vision in the Academy is to create an environment that allows people to reach their highest level on and off the pitch. We provide a games programme that is challenging and pits the boys against some of the best players of their age in the country and overseas. In the office where I'm sat, there are pennants from the likes of Bayern Munich, Juventus, AC Milan and Deportivo – these are the clubs we've played against, some of the best in Europe.

The Academy and first team are more closely aligned than they've ever been and the playing philosophy is consistent across the board, with Mark Bonner having been a key component in implementing that while he was in the role I'm now in. He's carried those same beliefs into his role as head coach and the results have been fantastic. I know when our Academy lads go into that first-team environment it will be a fluid transition. I can't speak highly enough of the first-team staff and players and the culture they have created. Being around people like Paul Digby, Greg Taylor, Harrison Dunk – they're great examples for our young players to learn from.

6. Ex-U's flying the flag
Matt Ramsay

Across Cambridge's relegation season from the Football League and our first in the Conference, Dave Kitson scored thirty-seven times in the Championship for Reading. Each goal was a cause for celebration among the U's faithful, who take pride in the achievements of former Abbey heroes.

The whole Cambridge team scored only thirty-nine times as League status was lost in 2005, which shows what disparate levels we and our former forward were operating at, but I love the fact we can take joy from the success of those who once donned the amber and black.

So long as United don't make an improbable rise to the upper echelons of English football, we will never be a club able to retain our very best players. Individual star names have made it, cementing their place in the wider sporting consciousness through their achievements after leaving the U's.

This is something United fans take great pleasure in, following the top flight vicariously through the exploits of Dion Dublin, John Ruddy and Kitson, among others. Each has graced the Premier League, which – though once close – Cambridge are not likely ever to do.

Of course, this works both ways. For all the pride at seeing Michael Morrison carve out a long career for himself in the second tier having cut his teeth under Rob Newman and Jimmy Quinn, there is that pained 'if only' feeling at seeing Jermaine Easter transforming himself into one of the hottest properties in the country at Wycombe.

Players don't even have to move to bigger clubs in order for us to bask in the warm glow of their triumphs. 'Goal Coulson' became an improbably common terrace shout when our Josh rattled in five goals in nine weeks as Leyton Orient won the National League in 2019, and there was rightful delight that such a wonderful servant of the club could enjoy success after departing.

Whenever we ordain a new hero at the Abbey, we do so in the knowledge that one day they will probably leave us, but as much as we love our club, we are capable of bestowing our best wishes on the individual. That's something to be proud of.

7. Dion Dublin
Liam Daish

When I met up with Dion again at Coventry, nothing had changed from our Cambridge days. He'd been to Manchester United, he was captain at Coventry when I signed, but he was still good old Dion who liked a laugh, liked a pint. On top of that, he was a very good player, someone you'd want in your team.

We came to the Abbey after we'd both been released by bigger clubs and we saw Cambridge as our second chance. Dion was initially viewed as a centre-half so it's not like he arrived as this ready-made striker; he had to work at it. There was the likes of George Reilly, Laurie Ryan and John Taylor keeping him out of the side.

But Dion had this athleticism, he was great in the air, he was technically a good finisher – if he lacked anything back then it was probably just a little bit of toughness, believe it or not. The environment we were in toughens you up because we had to do whatever it took in order to break into the first team, so you felt that pressure to step up and Dion rose to that challenge.

I remember his hat-trick against Peterborough – that was when Dion really announced himself. He was up against a really experienced couple of centre-halves and they just couldn't deal with him. People realised then just how huge his potential was because he could do a bit of everything.

He would come in for a bit of special attention sometimes from the opposition and I never minded a bit of confrontation or conflict so I was happy to help him out, but after a while Dion learned to look after himself – don't you worry about that!

When he got his million-pound move to Man United, that was the reward for his hard work. He had a good team around him at Cambridge but Dion was always going to be the one who got the big move. He's a bit of hero there and he deserves that for what he achieved at Cambridge and what he's done since. I like listening to his analysis on the game, he's done all sorts on TV – he's basically the face of the BBC! – and now he's on the board at Cambridge. He's experienced life at bigger clubs but Dion knows where it all started for him and it's in his personality to want to give something back.

8. Election to the Football League

'I expect to be in the Football League during the term of my contract.' Those were the words of Bill Leivers after he took the reins at Southern League Cambridge United in 1967. With the U's having failed in three election bids already, it was a bold statement of intent. Leivers, an FA Cup winner with Manchester City in his playing days, was not a man to shirk a challenge and nor was he afraid to position himself as one of the primary drivers of the club's ambitions to join the elite.

'It was a comfortable club,' explains Leivers, who, having broken his nose five times, his elbow twice and his ankle once in ten years at City, was not all that attached to the notion of being comfortable. 'They probably had ambition but they had absolutely no idea how to get anywhere. I had to take that club by the scruff of the neck and stand it on its feet.'

Even with the formidable Leivers at the helm, United suffered further setbacks in 1968 and 69, although the jump from two votes to sixteen off the back of a league and cup double afforded plenty of room for optimism. 'Although we are disappointed at not gaining election, these sixteen votes have given us tremendous hope for the future,' Leivers said at the time. 'We must now keep winning our competitions and eventually we must be recognised.'

Keep winning they did, with a second consecutive Southern League title secured in 1970 to send United into the election process brimming with confidence. Chairman John Woolley and his board, including Reg Smart, Dave Ruston and Paddy Harris, left no stone unturned in their attempts to win favour with the League's member clubs, with a public relations firm appointed to aid the cause.

The Football League AGM took place on 30th May at London's Café Royal, when the United squad were on a tour of Germany. Incumbents Bradford Park Avenue received only seventeen votes, leaving open a spot that seemed destined to be filled by either Cambridge or Wigan. It was United who got the nod, securing thirty-one votes to Wigan's eighteen.

Speaking from the Wesseling Hotel in Germany, a characteristically pragmatic Leivers said: 'I never doubted we would get in. Our performances over the past two seasons made sure we would be elected. Now we have got to show that we merited the members' decision.'

9. John Docherty
Tom Finney

John Docherty was a good football man. Him and Ron Atkinson had success together and when Ron left Doc took over and we went up into the Second Division; that's when things got a lot harder. Doc did a great job to consolidate at that level and maybe doesn't get the credit he deserves.

We were playing big clubs – the likes of Newcastle, Chelsea and West Ham – but we all thought we belonged there. We had good players who weren't out of place in that league, people like Dave Stringer, Alan Biley, Steve Fallon and Steve Spriggs. Doc knew how to get the best out of us.

I used to be a forward and when I was coming into my late twenties, I was slowing down a bit; I couldn't get the other side of the defender, so Doc moved me back into midfield. I could do a bit of both sides of the game – I could win the ball and read the second knocks and I could also play. That move into midfield gave me a longer career by probably two or three years and that was down to Johnny Doc.

He knew the game and he knew his players. He did a similar thing with Jamie Murray, who started as a left-winger but Doc moved him to left-back and he became a different player. He was quite clever, Doc. And he wasn't shy if he had to tell people when they were going wrong or if he had to make changes.

When the rule came in where the home team keeps the gate money, that made it even more difficult for a club like Cambridge and it became a bit of a struggle. Doc had to do what he needed to do to keep Cambridge in that league. We used to sit in a bit more and didn't score as many goals, so maybe that's why sometimes he doesn't get the credit he ought to.

We really struggled with the managers who came after Doc. I remember coming back from Brentford and scoring the goal that got John Ryan his first win. Maybe if the club had stuck with John Doc, he would've stopped the rot. The club would probably have gone down but I think Doc might have got them back up again. You can't fault the job he did.

10. Living the dream
Luke Chadwick

My dream was always to play for Cambridge United. My first experience of going to a live game was at Cambridge. That's where I fell in love with football, at the Abbey, so close to the action you could smell the turf.

Wherever I've gone in my career I've always kept up with the club. At Man United I would have been checking the Cambridge score on Teletext. I had a spell at Norwich where I was injured for quite a bit and I went to a lot of games when we were struggling in the Conference.

I'd get the DVDs they put out, like the Great Escape one where Robbie Simpson got a hat-trick up at Northwich. I always tried to stay in touch as much as I could.

As I got towards the end of my career, I knew I had to make the move happen. I met up with Karl Robinson and, funnily enough, Gary Waddock, who was the assistant at MK Dons at the time, and I told them what my dream was. They were taken aback but Karl was fantastic with me. I contacted Jez George, met with him and Richard Money and we got it sorted out.

Richard introduced me to the players and I obviously knew who they all were because I'd been keeping track all season. It was incredible to be stood in front of the likes of Luke Berry and Josh Coulson, who I'd only really known from watching them play, and suddenly we're meeting as team-mates. It was quite a surreal experience for everyone in that dressing room. The calibre of the people there was just incredible. That's what got us to Wembley and beating Gateshead to get back into the Football League, which was huge for the club.

I remember years before that walking past the Guildhall in Cambridge telling my wife and kids that one day I'd be stood up there as a Cambridge player celebrating promotion. That was a dream that came true and I'm so proud to be able to say that.

The party back at the Abbey, what I can remember of it, was great. My missus likes to remind me I got back about 2 a.m. and was singing the Luke Berry song in her face. Memories like that stay with you forever.

11. The pre-match ritual
Julian Roberts

Picture the scene: it's around 1 p.m. on any given Saturday. You're sat in The Dobblers Inn. Or The Cambridge Blue. Or The White Swan. Or The Cornerhouse. Or wherever your pre-game pub of choice might be. You've maybe had a few beers and that Saturday afternoon buzz is just creeping in. Another game at the Abbey; no matter how bad United's fortunes are, it's always there to be cherished.

The early kick-off is on; some endlessly boring Premier League game you've had a small flutter on just to extract some sort of joy out of it. You're looking around at those same faces you see every week, those same faces you've spent so much time with and been through so much with. Those many, many low points that make those few highs so much sweeter. That unspoken 'why do we put ourselves through this' bond, but none of you would change it for the world.

The conversation is about who should play today. Or what the score will be. Or where someone ended up after last week's away day. And then it's what trains are we on for next week's.

A big call goes up. The shouting dies to a murmur and a game of pool is dramatically halted as someone reads out the line-up with a familiar mix of happiness and scepticism. There's probably a little moment of surprise at someone's inclusion: 'Corr's playing?!'

A few more beers down, you take a stab in the dark at a six-team accumulator that will never come in, but it's nearly 3 p.m. on a Saturday so it's going on.

'One more?' – it's a rhetorical question. You see it off quicker than it arrives and set off for a stroll down Newmarket Road, limbering up en route as if you might be starting on the left wing. The sight of the ground from the bridge still gives you a rush. Every time. Past the Common, a few hellos outside the turnstiles, and into the ground at 2.58 p.m. Head swimming, anticipation building, those heroes in amber and black ready to make you proud.

This is my pre-match ritual, and it might be nothing like yours, but we each have one; it's what makes us feel a part of something bigger, something that really does mean more.

12. Wilf Mannion

It's hard to propose a modern-day comparison for just how much of a coup it was for Cambridge to sign Wilf Mannion without incurring a great deal of incredulity. If you were to say it was on a par with Lionel Messi joining the U's that might seem like a stretch, and perhaps it is, but not to the extent you would imagine.

Mannion is regarded as one of the finest talents in English football history, described by the legendary Billy Shankly as having "every quality imaginable." It mattered little that he plied his trade in an era when defenders could get away with borderline assault, they simply could not get close enough to touch him.

He won twenty-six caps for England in an international career that followed his time on the front lines in the Second World War. Mannion scored eleven goals for his country, including one at the 1950 World Cup at the famed Maracana against Chile. It was with Middlesbrough that he made his name, racking up 110 goals in 368 appearances. A statue of his diminutive figure – Mannion was just five feet five inches tall – stands proudly outside the Riverside Stadium.

Having fallen out of love with the game, Mannion announced his retirement in 1954 before changing his mind and signing for Hull City in a spell that was cut short by a Football League ban imposed for articles he had written exposing illegal payments offered to him by an unnamed club.

Cast into the wilderness and nursing a renewed desire to continue playing, the 36-year-old Mannion had a brief stint with Poole Town before United manager Bert Johnson seized his chance and lured the man they nicknamed 'The Golden Boy' to the Abbey.

The Cambridge Daily News edition of 25th June, 1956 proudly proclaimed: 'Wilf Mannion, one of the greatest inside-forwards of the post-war era, will play in United colours next season.' Mannion scored twenty-two goals in seventy-nine outings for the U's, eschewing the option to return to the Football League once his ban was lifted. He died in 2000 at the age of eighty-one.

The club will never see his ilk again.

13. Wembley heroics
Ryan Donaldson

Just before we went up to collect the FA Trophy, when we were gathered out of sight of the fans, Richard Money said to us: 'Make sure we come back here.' I remember it vividly.

The Trophy was something for us to enjoy but we didn't want it to be the highlight of our season. It helped we were playing a team from a lower division and we expected to win, which obviously we did. When you score at Wembley, it doesn't sink in during the game. The moment of realisation came when I left the lounge afterwards and walked down the steps, looking at the pitch and the magnitude of this huge empty stadium – it hit me then that I'd done it at Wembley.

We had a strange period at the end of the season with a poor run of results and we had an issue with our goalkeepers getting injured. We were doing shape work before the final game of the season against Gateshead and we had Josh Coulson in goal. I was thinking surely we can't be going into the play-offs with Josh in goal – I'm sure he'd have done a job, but still! Richard changed the system for the play-off final, which was brave, but he deserves huge credit for switching it around at half-time because it turned the game in our favour and we were soon ahead. When I hit the cross in for Hughesy I thought it was going to be too close to the keeper, but Hughesy anticipated it and got us up and running.

When it came to the free-kick, me and Hughesy wanted it. We both marked out our run-ups and still hadn't decided at that point. He'd scored one up at Tamworth from a similar range and if it was up to him, he'd have taken it. We were both stood there ready to take it when I said: 'No, I've got this.' When it left my boot, I knew I'd hit it well – when I saw it clear the wall, I was already getting set to run off and celebrate. There's that famous photo of the pile-on with Champs on top. It was a brilliant moment.

I've still got my shirt and boots from that day. Promotion was the culmination of a year's work for me, but it was the reward for so many more years of work from so many other people and that's why it was emotional for me; seeing how much it meant to people who had been there years, people like Matt Walker, Jez George, Mark Bonner, and seeing Josh Coulson going over to his dad in the crowd – that set me off! It was just an incredible day.

UNITED ENJOY STAGS PARTY

Cambridge United secured promotion to Division Three for the first time in their history as Ronnie Walton hit the winner in a thrilling 3-2 triumph over Mansfield Town.

In a winner-takes-all clash, it was Bill Leivers' men who claimed the honours at a packed and raucous Abbey Stadium, where United twice fought back from behind to seal the points that wrapped up a maiden Football League promotion just three years after being elected.

Jim McCaffrey's header was cancelled out by Walton and, while Dudley Roberts restored the Stags' advantage, Bobby Ross converted a penalty to ensure it was honours even at the break.

Walton was ultimately the hero, his brilliantly executed first-time effort from Brian Greenhalgh's cross settling matters after 67 minutes.

It caps a fine campaign from Leivers' side and a dramatic improvement on last season's mid-table finish, with goal machine Greenhalgh leading the way.

With United having lost four of their first five games, it also represents a stunning turnaround and the U's are now braced for third-tier football.

Key players

Brian Greenhalgh (45 appearances, 18 goals): Goals aplenty for the former Aston Villa forward, who is more fearsome than he looks.

Terry Eades (38 appearances, 1 goal): A rock at the back and a cool head under pressure, Eades oozes class.

David Lill (45 appearances, 12 goals): What an engine this man has! The midfielder's relentless running resulted in plenty of end product, too.

UNITED MAKING THEIR MARK AMONG ELITE

When Cambridge finally won election to the Football League back in 1970, manager Bill Leivers vowed to justify the decision of member clubs to welcome United into the elite.

With this hard-earned promotion, the U's have surely done just that. In only their third season in the League, Cambridge have proven themselves more than a match for clubs who had for many years closed ranks in order to keep them toiling away in the Southern League.

And with a magnificent crowd of 10,542 against Mansfield creating an electric atmosphere, the appetite for football in this fine city is clearly there.

Pos	Team	Pld	W	D	L	GF	GA	GD	Pts
1	Southport	46	26	10	10	71	48	+23	62
2	Hereford United	46	23	12	11	56	38	+18	58
3	Cambridge United	46	20	17	9	67	57	+10	57
4	Aldershot	46	22	12	12	60	38	+22	56
5	Newport County	46	22	12	12	64	44	+20	56
6	Mansfield Town	46	20	14	12	78	51	+27	54
7	Reading	46	17	18	11	51	38	+13	52

15. Moosenet Prediction League
Andy MPL

The Moosenet Prediction League began life on 6th March, 1999 with a 3-0 Cambridge United win at Exeter City. Thirty-seven predictors emailed their predictions. By the end of that first, partial season, eighty-four U's fans had joined the fun. Several who played in that maiden campaign are still predicting, an implausible twenty-two years on.

The MPL runs two seasons per year, with promotion and relegation between divisions. Across forty-five predicting seasons, there have been more than 125,000 predictions registered by 830 predictors (be they real, sock-puppets, one-off bored kids, 9-0 opposition jokers or Google bots).

You might expect U's fans to be optimistic – hopeful, I should say – in their nominations, but the stats don't really bear that out. Over those years, United have drawn just over a quarter of their games and won half of the remainder. MPL predictors have gone for the win 40.8 percent of the time, 4.4 percent more than they should, and for the draw 25.1 percent, which is 1.1 percentage points less often than that result has transpired.

Luke Berry's eye for goal has attracted the experts' ardour a dizzying 6,937 times, though Dave Kitson (for me the best striker in the MPL years) rewarded many of his 6,161 admirers in roughly half the games. In a distant third is Paul Mullin with 3,890, followed by Uche Ikpeazu, Tom Elliott, Tom Youngs, Michael Gash, Scott Rendell, Jevani Brown and Barry Corr.

The MPL keeps ticking along, with the winking light of a Raspberry Pi server on a dusty shelf to prove it, and I see no imminent danger of it perishing while the interest is there. I'd need seven years to train up an apprentice to succeed me anyway.

I have a tiny but very select set of friends from the old days, but I also have a hundred-and-something like-minded crazy people who I think of as… not friends exactly… maybe… people who might do me physical harm if I let the MPL die. And that's the important thing.

16. Marvin the Moose
Dale 'Moose' Collett

Swansea have a swan, Leicester have a fox, Millwall have a lion – people must wonder why in the world Cambridge United have a moose as a mascot! It's the kind of story that can only happen at a club like Cambridge.

It all began back in 1989 when I was coming back from a lads' holiday in Benidorm. We had stayed up all night and had an early flight back to Stansted, where we arrived beer-soaked and somewhat the worse for wear. The plan was always to go to the first game of the season, which was Grimsby away.

We headed straight up there and arrived just before kick-off on a hot summer's day. It was in the era of all the inflatables and there was that typical buzz of excitement you get at the opening game of the season.

I saw some mates on the terraces and they went to give me a hug but I hadn't showered since the night before and just came out with the line: 'Don't come near me, I smell like a moose.' I'd never said it before but it just came to me in the moment. I don't know why I picked a moose.

There was a real party atmosphere that day and it became a joke on the terraces, with people singing moose songs, putting the goalkeeper off by shouting 'moose', and from there it started this sort of moose-mania.

It's amazing how it took off. I was almost embarrassed by it because I couldn't fathom how it had become such a big thing. Suddenly the players were 'doing the moose', waving their hands by the side of their heads like antlers. They did that on the Guildhall balcony celebrating promotion; we chanted 'give us a moose' and they all did it – even the chairman and John Beck.

It didn't stop there; we had replica shirts with moose embedded in them, there were 'moose on tour' t-shirts. I think the whole phenomenon was just a case of timing. Marvin will outlive us all and it's lovely to know that I'll leave something behind at a club that means so much to me.

17. Tom Finney
Keith Lockhart

If Tom Finney was playing now, he'd be in the Premier League. Easily. He was like N'Golo Kante at Chelsea – taking the ball off the back four, picking a pass, winning tackles. That's exactly how Tom was. To me, he's one of the best Cambridge players ever.

When I first came to Cambridge, Tom had just dropped back from a forward into midfield. If he had made that move earlier in his career he would definitely have gone on to a bigger club in the top division. He had all the qualities.

In those days it was more like a war on the pitch. You could get away with tackles you wouldn't get away with now, and Tom would certainly stand up for himself. He's got this hard man reputation but he was, first and foremost, a really good footballer. I was a young lad breaking into the team and he was brilliant to play with and learn from. He helped me no end.

He would get kicked – and, fair enough, he'd kick a few people back – but he would never moan. Tom would always just get on with the job at hand, he never complained. He never really played any differently either, and that was even the case in training. John Ryan, for some unknown reason, got rid of Tom and then obviously he came back but Tom just kept on playing his own game and he never let anything like that bother him.

I don't think Tom realises the regard he's held in and quite what he achieved. This is a guy who has played at a World Cup. I used to say to him: 'Tom, you've played at Wembley against people like Kevin Keegan, and my hero Malcolm Macdonald' – he just brushed it off like it was nothing. I was more excited for him than he was.

But he and his family are the nicest people you could wish to meet. He's one of my best friends in football. I was only fifteen when I moved down to Cambridge and his family have been great to me over the years. I'm godfather to his son, Nick. I consider them family. He was a quality player and he's a quality mate to me. I can't give higher praise than that.

18. The intrigue
Doug Shulman

My dad took me to my first ever United game in 1982, a friendly at Haverhill Rovers. United won 10-0. I thought it must be like that all the time, so every time I went to a game there was this sense of anticipation that something remarkable might happen.

I now know that Cambridge don't win 10-0 every week, but there's still that intrigue of never quite knowing what you're going to get. That's what I love.

I've only seen United win promotion five times in thirty-nine years but every season you start off thinking, 'Is this going to be the year?' The answer is usually no, of course, but you just never know.

Look at the 2020-21 season – I sat there in pre-season and thought mid-table would be a sign of solid progress under Mark Bonner, and if we had a really good season we might just sneak into the play-offs. And yet there we were towards the end of the season sitting top of the table, with a chance of actually winning it.

Yet all throughout that experience you have these worries about whether we'll fall away and it comes back to that intrigue and anticipation of just not knowing. To get to the point of achieving promotion – and I had the privilege of actually being there to witness it – sums up how unpredictable it all is.

You go to games where we could win 5-0 or lose 5-0, we could get relegated or promoted. It's part of the excitement of being a fan, having no specific expectations but feeling like anything could happen. It means when you do have a season like that promotion one it's even more enjoyable. One really good season erases all of the mind-numbing mediocrity of what has gone before.

The promotion in 2013-14 meant even more; it banished the pain and anguish of the past nine years. There's no feeling quite like it. It's those moments that keep you going as a fan and make it all worthwhile.

19. Lionel Perez
Dave Kitson

Lionel Perez was without a doubt the biggest single influence by any one player on my career and on my mentality as a player, bar none. Nobody opened my eyes more to the attitude that's needed to succeed than Lionel Perez.

He embodied, in the way he trained, the way he carried himself and the way he played, a resilient spirit and absolute determination to succeed. What really struck me is that he had the knowledge that he was bloody good. I always wanted that and he instilled that in me for when I went to Reading.

I got there and thought, 'Yes, I'm good and I will be a success.' People confuse that with arrogance, they probably have done with Lionel, but it's an absolutely unshakable belief that you are, for whatever level you're playing at, as good as it gets. And he showed me the road to go down to get there, and how to do it and what you have to do to succeed. He was the best.

If somebody were to give me the reins of a football team tomorrow, my first call would probably be to Lionel asking if he wanted to be my goalkeeping coach.

I've got nothing but respect for Lionel. I've got a lot of respect for a lot of people, but he's my number one, without wanting to be too corny. I think about him a lot when I'm applying my own experiences to certain situations because he always used to do the right thing.

I'd go to him a lot at the Abbey Stadium; whenever we were going to get changed or going off to train, he always had a word for me and I think he wanted to help me. We'd bump into each other, whether by design or coincidence, but he never just talked for the sake of talking to me; he always had something to say. I always used to come away from a conversation with Lionel thinking, 'Bloody hell, that was interesting,' or, 'I learnt something there.' Genuinely.

I don't speak to him enough; he's a great guy. He's been a massive influence on me and he still is, without even knowing it.

20. John Haasz
John Haasz Jr

My dad was in the resistance fighting during the revolution against Russian control over Hungary. When the Russians sent in the troops, my dad's life was on the line – he was in a firing squad but he got saved. He was only twenty-two when he had to leave the country.

He managed to escape and come to England, where all those who had fled had to report to a police station. They asked him what he needed and he told them: 'I came here with nothing; I don't need anything – I'll just go and get a job.' And that's exactly what he did.

Because of what was going on, Hungarian footballers were banned from playing for three years by FIFA. Dad had played for Hungary Under-21s but now he could only play at amateur level, so he turned out for colliery teams and they paid quite well. He had a job with British Ropes, who made steel roping for bridges, and they asked him to play for them but he said he was getting better money playing for the colliery team, so they sacked him!

He wasn't the biggest – he was only about five foot eight – and he wasn't stocky, but he was a tough man. There was one time he broke his ribs and carried on playing. I think what he'd been through had toughened him up.

When he was at Cambridge, we lived straight across from the ground on Newmarket Road in a bungalow that belonged to the club. We used to play on the pitch but I think I only ever went to one match. Dad had a part-time job tyre fitting, which he took up again when he moved up to Doncaster to be with my mum.

Dad was very confident and strong-willed, he loved his family and he was a very good cook. He loved football and he spoke about it constantly; he'd tell us the same stories over and over again. We did wonder if he was exaggerating sometimes but then we'd hear the same stories from other people and we knew he wasn't making it up.

There was a newspaper cutting that said my dad was the first Hungarian to play in British football. It makes me proud to know he's so highly thought of, especially at Cambridge. We miss him.

21. Making ends meet
Rob Newman

I'd describe the situation I came into at Cambridge as a challenge. The club was in administration and in that first pre-season training session we had a handful of contracted pros and about thirty-five trialists. As a manager you just want a fair crack – just simple stuff like having enough footballs to train with, or having bibs the same colour, or enough cones to lay out for drills. Sometimes we'd wonder if there was enough petrol in the minibus. It wasn't ideal, but you always think you can overcome adversity.

I had Tony Spearing with me as my assistant and he worked for nothing for the first month. I phoned him and told him I needed help and he was happy to get involved. It helped me immensely having him as a sounding board, he could always put a smile on my face if I was feeling down and he had a great rapport with the players. He was top drawer.

We never had a fixed training ground, so we would be at one college one day and then another one for the next two. When we did get to train on those pitches it was like a bowling green, but on some days if it was raining and they didn't want us to train there we'd end up on Coldham's Common and we'd have to take all the kit down there, including the goals. We'd mark out the pitch with poles and jumpers. It was all character building.

The budget was halved but we managed to be competitive and finish mid-table. We had players who had been discarded by other clubs and we were operating in really tough circumstances but there was not one time they came off the pitch and I felt they hadn't tried for me and for the club. You can't ask for more than that. We had good characters and some decent players, the likes of Mark Peters, Andy Duncan, Rob Wolleaston and Courtney Pitt. They had a good grounding and they got on with the job, despite everything. The younger lads looked up to them.

The fans were great at Cambridge, especially away from home. They used to sing 'Buzz Lightyear's Amber Army,' which people said I should take as a compliment because he's a superhero, but I never let my daughter watch a Toy Story movie! I had great banter with the supporters and I have a lot of affection for the time I had there. It's a different footballing universe to the one I'm in now but I'm glad I had the experience.

22. Richard Money

How can you fail to love a man who draws inspiration for his post-match interviews from Hollywood blockbusters? Those listening to Richard Money on BBC Radio Cambridgeshire following a 1-0 win over Hereford in October 2013 found themselves transported back to ancient Rome, with Dickie Dosh cast in the role of the titular Gladiator who, having laid waste to all comers, asks of his baying audience with evident disdain: 'Are you not entertained?'

Money's palpable irritation and characteristic truculence made for a performance far more compelling than Russell Crowe's. Alas, there is no Academy Award for Best Performance on Local Radio.

But Money, who won the European Cup with Liverpool in his playing days, was not always so spiky and, much like a supine hedgehog, did have occasion to show his softer side.

It was that more charming version of Money who rejoiced with supporters at the Abbey after he had led the club back to the Football League with a 2-1 play-off final victory over Gateshead at Wembley in 2014. Leading a rendition of 'Tell me ma to put the champagne on ice,' posing for photos and even breaking into a smile, Money proved himself a lovable character after all.

There was yet more joy to come from his three-year tenure, an FA Cup run that accounted for old tormentors Luton Town and culminated in a lucrative replay at Old Trafford putting the U's in the international spotlight as Money's amber heroes gave Louis van Gaal's under-fire Manchester United an almighty scare.

Money departed in November 2015 and did so with his head held high, declaring in a statement released by the League Managers Association: 'I am incredibly proud of my achievements with Cambridge United. I would like to thank the fans for sticking with the team and supporting me during the past three years.

'It has been a privilege to have been part of the success of this great club.'

23. That play-off final commentary

As Cambridge United's play-off final against Gateshead headed deep into stoppage time, the U's were edging ever closer to ending a nine-year exile from the Football League. Among the many thousands of Cambridge fans at Wembley, two were duty-bound to keep their cool in the sweltering heat. This is how Mark Johnson and Doug Shulman called the last few moments of that game on BBC Radio Cambridgeshire, as agony turned to ecstasy...

Doug: 'We're now into the one hundredth minute of this match, Mark.'

Johnno: 'How much longer? Peter Banks, only you know. He's the referee.'

Doug: 'Come on my son, put that whistle to your mouth.'

Johnno: '2-1 to the U's, tenth minute of stoppage time. Oh, United, why do you do this to us?'

Doug: 'He's still playing on. He's playing on, the referee.'

Johnno: 'Ball goes forward, Cunnington challenges and has won a throw for United deep in Gateshead territory, which United will be in no rush... Luke Chadwick just asks the referee how long to go.'

Doug: 'He is, and he's taking his time, Harrison Dunk. The referee just taking another little glance at his watch. He wants to carry on, the referee.'

Johnno: 'I don't.'

Doug: 'Can't be much longer, Mark! Please blow, referee!'

Johnno: 'Throw-in down the line, finding Cunnington. Head for the corner – that's what he does, looks to block it away. Another throw to United... it matters not! And United are back in the Football League. Relegated in 2005, they've done it at last.'

24. Lindsay 'Wolfie' Smith
Derrick Christie

Lindsay got his cult status because the fans could identify with him. He always gave it everything he had and the people watching from the stands love that. Sometimes people question if players are doing enough, but with Lindsay there was never any doubt he would give his all, and a little bit more. He had the beard as well and a bit of an image to go with the cult hero thing.

He made his debut at Colchester United when he was only sixteen. He was there for five years and then got involved in a contract dispute. He didn't go on strike but he knew what he wanted and what he felt he deserved. He's a strong character so he stuck by his guns and ended up getting a move to Cambridge United.

You only need to look at the managers who signed him to know what Lindsay was all about. Bobby Moncur, who was a defender, signed him at Plymouth and they went on to the semi-final of the FA Cup; he was signed by George Graham at Millwall and did a good job there; he was signed by Ron Atkinson at Cambridge, Chris Turner the second time – these people all recognised what qualities Lindsay had.

I should say that Lindsay didn't like training – he got bored. He's an intelligent guy and he didn't like the repetition. It's funny because when I talk to Lindsay now he says he misses the training and the running – he never used to like running! He did as little as possible. He's one of the few players who I've met where he was nothing great in training, but as soon as he crossed that line in a match he was fantastic.

He had a lot of skill. There's a famous clip of Maradona doing keepy-uppies where he boots the ball twenty yards up in the air each time – I've seen Lindsay do that about fifteen times on the trot. He's very down to earth, very understated, so he's not one for talking up how good he was or what he did in his career.

The thing is now I'm going to have to tell him I've said all this next time we speak. I'll buy a copy of the book and give it to him as a laugh.

25. The Newmarket Road End
Will Hunting-Jones

One of my first memories of the Newmarket Road End is a game against Bradford City in 1991. We needed to win to get promoted and in the second half we were attacking towards that stand. I was stood in the Habbin and when the own goal went in that won us promotion the whole stadium went crazy, but I remember looking over at the Newmarket Road End and it was just something else – I knew then that I had to get in there. The season after that I started going in the NRE and it soon became like a second home to me.

It's just an iconic stand. Most football clubs have had their own version throughout the years, but ours is rare in that it's still standing in its original form. They don't build stands like that now, with the roof so low that the sound just bounces straight back off it and creates a deafening noise. And we've now got 'Amber Army' emblazoned on the wall at back, so it really feels like it belongs to the supporters.

It's an incredible place. Some of the best memories of my life come from being in there, going crazy celebrating goals. When that place gets rocking, there is nowhere else like it. I think of the play-off games we've had at the Abbey, the atmosphere created behind that goal. I remember the Manchester United game in the FA Cup and being stood on one of the barriers and soaking in this electric atmosphere.

Thousands of people have stood on that terrace over the years and in so many cases life has led them to move on, whether it's university or marriage or a job, and their relationship with the football club has changed. But the memories will always come flooding back as soon as you see it; even just seeing a picture of it, your mind instantly goes to all of the things you've experienced there.

That's a rare thing in life, to have a specific place where so many memories reside, and so many happy memories. That's what gives the Newmarket Road End its aura – it embodies a living, breathing history of the club and its fans. It's a special place and, whatever the future holds for the club in terms of the stadium, it deserves to be preserved in some way.

26. Steve Butler
Matthew Gooding

As the world's worst glory hunter, my love affair with Cambridge United began as the halcyon days of the John Beck era were disappearing from view. By the time I started visiting the Abbey on a regular basis, in 1993-94, Shaggy and Dion had long since departed, and though Steve Claridge saw the error of his ways and briefly returned from Luton, the closest thing we had to a star striker was Steve Butler.

Butler had been signed the previous season from Watford and was supposed to score the goals to save us from relegation. That didn't happen, and as a result he was not a popular figure on the terraces. His languid playing style and the fact he looked a bit like an off-duty financial advisor probably didn't help, but it was his propensity to miss simple chances that seemed to grate on a lot of people, including my dad.

But for some reason, perhaps simply because he was wearing the number nine shirt, I took an instant shine to Butler, and after one particularly dour performance a bet was struck; if Butler scored a hat-trick before the end of the season, dad would buy me a season ticket for the following campaign.

For a long time it looked like dad's cash was safe, but then something strange happened; Butler's performances began to improve, apparently aided by visits to an osteopath to ease a long-standing back problem. Over a memorable Easter weekend, he netted a treble against Leyton Orient, as my disbelieving dad and I watched on, before netting five goals away at Exeter on Easter Monday. Having scored five times in the first three quarters of the season, he ended the term with a run of sixteen goals in eleven games, including another hat-trick against Cardiff. Despite this hat-trick of hat-tricks, I only got one season ticket.

Butler scored regularly for the following season and a half, striking up a deadly partnership with Carlo Corazzin which continued to flourish even as the team around them diminished, and another relegation was endured. He eventually left us for Gillingham, claiming the drive from his home in Kent was aggravating his back. It was a betrayal that took me some time to recover from, but they say you always remember your first love and to this day he retains a special place in my heart.

UNITED PUT SEAL ON TITLE-WINNING SEASON

Ron Atkinson's classy Cambridge United wrapped up their Division Four title-winning season in style with a 3-1 victory at Aldershot.

With promotion having been secured after the 3-0 win over Doncaster Rovers, the championship was sealed courtesy of a 0-0 draw at Stockport County.

And United put the icing on the cake with a victory lap against the lowly Shots, their goals-scored tally rising to 87 in the process.

United's swashbuckling style has won many admirers this season, with the Abbey transformed into a fortress as the U's smashed in 57 goals and conceded only 18 in 23 matches on home soil.

Just two sides left Cambridge with maximum points, while Swansea City were the only team in the division to do the double over Atkinson's charges.

A stunning debut season from Tom Finney and the emergence of young forward Alan Biley after last season's leg break were undoubtedly two key catalysts for a memorable campaign.

> **Key players**
>
> Alan Biley (46 appearances, 19 goals): Biley was a loss to the U's after his injury blow last term, but he made up for lost time with a joint-record goals haul for United.
>
> Tom Finney (40 appearances, 16 goals): The Northern Ireland midfielder is an incredible addition to United's ranks.
>
> Jim Hall (24 appearances, 15 goals): The best loan signing in United's history? The stats suggest he may well be.

U'S RON TO A WINNER

In Ron Atkinson, Cambridge United undoubtedly have one of the finest young managers in the Football League and keeping him must be the top priority if the club harbour ambitions to go even higher.

His larger-than-life personality off the pitch is matched by the eye-catching displays of his team on it, with United's attacking style a joy to behold this season, particularly at fortress Abbey.

Cambridge's last foray into the third tier was a short-lived affair as United suffered immediate relegation under Bill Leivers.

Atkinson will surely set his sights far higher for next season and, if the U's can keep hold of their star talents, they may just surprise a few once again.

Pos	Team	Pld	W	D	L	GF	GA	GD	Pts
1	Cambridge United	46	26	13	7	87	40	+47	65
2	Exeter City	46	25	12	9	70	46	+24	62
3	Colchester United	46	25	9	12	77	43	+33	59
4	Bradford City	46	23	13	10	78	51	+27	59
5	Swansea City	46	25	8	13	92	68	+24	58
6	Barnsley	46	23	9	14	62	39	+23	55
7	Watford	46	18	15	13	67	50	+17	51

28. Mark Bonner
Paul Barry

In my twenty years of being deeply involved with Cambridge United, I don't think I've seen anyone who has demonstrated as much passion and perspiration at this football club as Mark Bonner. I never take those things for granted. Although I would say he should probably learn when to take a break!

I first met Mark when he came back to the club from Southend. He was involved in our Academy and was spoken about very highly by the people he worked with. A couple of years after that I flew him over to the States, I took him to see how the Seattle Sounders operate and Mark really impressed me just as a human being.

He was an impressive individual but I can't say back then it crossed my mind that he would be our manager one day. When we had to let Colin Calderwood go and were looking at potential candidates, Mark was doing the best job interview possible by turning a team that had lost its passion, perspiration and belief into one that demonstrated all of those things.

My fellow director, Renford Sargent, made it clear that Mark wanted it permanently and it soon became very evident that he was the man for the job. He may only be in his thirties but he has a lot of experience of being around the first team and has seen what works and what doesn't. His man-management skills have really come to the fore – he is always clear and honest with his players.

He's already a club legend really for that miracle season, a season like no other – winning promotion behind closed doors. It meant more having Mark in charge. When you achieve something with homegrown talent, with people who are passionate about the club and will forever be linked to it, it's brilliant. He's one of our own.

I'm not one for people praising, but Mark Bonner is just a high-quality individual and I look forward to working with him for as long and far as he can take Cambridge. I'm sure he's got a bright future in football.

29. Bill Leivers

Vic Akers

Bill Leivers was the man who gave me the opportunity to play in the Football League when he signed me for Cambridge in 1971. He watched me play for Welling United at Cheltenham and then put an offer in and I got my move into the League at the age of twenty-two, which might be considered a little late but it was fantastic for me.

The club was new to the League at the time but it was ambitious and we had some very good players. We were a decent team under Bill and I had a great time at Cambridge. Bill himself was a gentle giant, he managed with a lot of dignity and he had a great deal of enthusiasm for the club and his players.

He could come down hard on players and get the big stick out when he needed to, but in the main he was a fair man and he treated us like men – unless anyone stepped out of line, then he would treat them as they behaved. Being a good lad, I was never in that situation!

It helps when you're playing under a manager who has been there and done it, and Bill had played at the highest level and won the FA Cup at Man City. You do have that much more respect for someone because of those achievements.

Given the background he had, I respected what he said and I learned a lot about the game under him. In football you never stop learning and I picked up a lot from Bill and of course went on to learn from someone like Arsene Wenger at Arsenal over more than twenty years at that club.

Bill led us to a promotion and there was a noticeable jump in the standard going up from the Fourth Division to the Third, but he gave us the belief that we were good enough to be there. He was good at instilling that belief in his players and we had belief in him too.

I've only crossed paths with Bill once since my time at Cambridge but he's a man I have a huge amount of respect for and someone I owe a debt of gratitude to for giving me the chance to fulfil my ambition of playing in the Football League.

30. Paul Wanless
Daniel Chillingworth

Wanny is Mr. Cambridge United. When you see the love and rapport he has with the fans and the club as a whole, it tells you all you need to know about what he did at the Abbey. The biggest thing I can say about Wanny – the King of the Abbey – is that he was an absolute animal on the pitch but a complete gentleman off it.

For the young lads in that Cambridge team in my era, we couldn't have had a better captain or role model than him. He treated all of us youngsters with respect but we always knew we had to meet his high standards when we stepped out onto that pitch. I used to clean Wanny's boots and that was a great grounding for me.

Even in training, he wouldn't take any prisoners. I remember in one pre-season game he got injured and they were trying to take him off on a stretcher, but he wanted to hobble back on and get on with it. That just summed him up; he would always give his all. But people should remember that Wanny could play as well. He was a really good passer of the ball and he scored a lot of goals for Cambridge. He was a beast in both boxes.

I look back on my own Cambridge career with a lot of pride. That was a very good team that myself and the likes of Adam Tann managed to break into. You had people like David Preece, Neil Mustoe, Andy Duncan and Alex Russell, with Roy McFarland in charge. To be around people like that in training every day has such a positive effect on you, not only from a football point of view but also for life lessons and values. I learned a lot of really important things, especially from Wanny.

The overriding thing for me when it comes to Wanny is, yes, he was a great footballer and he's a club legend, but he's a great man more than anything else. I was privileged to play alongside him and even more so to call him a friend now. We still play golf together and it's nice to be able to share some stories of the past with a man who is undoubtedly Cambridge United through and through.

31. Being club captain
Greg Taylor

You're seen as a bit of a role model when you're captain. Leading the team out on a match day is brilliant but there's a lot stuff that comes with it which people don't see, so it does increase your workload quite a bit.

The type of captain you are depends on the individual. Some like to lead purely by their performances, with others it's more vocal – I like to think I do a bit of both. The context of the game can dictate which type of leader you need to be at any point, but the role comes with a lot of responsibility. You need to set the standard and deliver the key messages before and after the game. If you feel something needs to be said at half-time, you have to be able to stand up and deliver that.

There are times that being captain can make you a target. If you get caught speaking to the manager for too long, there's always a bit of banter from the boys. I've found it easy with the team-mates I've had at Cambridge; they respect me and the job I have to do, so I'm fine with any stick that goes along with it.

To lead the team to a promotion was massive. You look back on some games and the things you've said at half-time or during games which have had the desired impact and it does give you a huge sense of pride.

Then you've got situations like we faced at Harrogate, which was the most ridiculous game I've ever played in. It was a difficult dressing room at half-time because obviously there was a lot to be said, but I had to take responsibility for my own part in that. You have to tread carefully but you're still well within your rights to be dishing it out to try to drive the standards up.

Of course we had some doubts creeping in after that game, but as players and particularly as captain you have to control your emotions. I knew I had to help lift the mood, and you do that by being positive, by letting go of whatever's happened before and making it business as usual. We took the pressure out of the situation as much as possible and you saw how we produced when we needed to against Grimsby. That was a proud day and we'll all have some special memories to take away from that.

32. A community that cares
Connor O'Reilly

My love and dedication to the U's is well known and evidenced by the appearance of both myself and my Cambridge/Chile flag at grounds up and down the country. But amid the stresses and strains of a global pandemic, I made my battle against my mental health struggles just as conspicuous.

In that dark time, I faced a battle I did not know how to win. My anxiety and depression were spiralling and I had no idea how to cope with it.

I've always struggled. I started following United when I was fifteen, an age when the mind plays cruel tricks on you. Every time I went up to the Abbey, I stood alone. What I failed to realise until I got older was that I was in a crowd of 4,000 people, all of whom would be going through something, from the highs like a promotion at work to the lows of losing a loved one.

Fast forward a few years and coronavirus struck, taking us all in its grip and removing from us so much of what we love, not least of all the ability to watch football matches live in stadiums. It was hard for me, as it was for many people, but it was also a turning point.

Enough was enough. I didn't want to live in silence anymore and I opened up, penning a 1,500-word article on my love for the club and how it had helped me through my struggles.

The reaction was astonishing. From my family and friends to colleagues at work, it was all so positive. And then there was the response from the club, which was perhaps the most amazing part of it. Over Christmas in 2020, I spoke with Mark Bonner as he called season ticket holders and had a chat about mental health. I also talked to Godric Smith and Harry Darling about what is a really important issue to me, and obviously to the club too.

I've always been proud of this club, but this experience showed me that Cambridge United is much more than just a place to go and watch football every Saturday: it's a community that genuinely cares. I'm proud to be a U.

33. A club I'd be proud to play for... again
Michael Morrison

I got my break at Cambridge after the club had been relegated from the Football League and the Academy had been disbanded. That was obviously a terrible time for the club, but as a seventeen-year-old it afforded me an opportunity to play sooner than might otherwise have been the case.

I played alongside some experienced pros, people like Andy Duncan, Wayne Hatswell and Mark Albrighton, then there was Mark Peters, who could head the ball as far as he could kick it, and he really looked after me. Playing in a back three I had some protection but I felt ready to play and compete physically at that level even at that young age.

There were a few clubs who took me on trial and I went up to Newcastle when Glenn Roeder was manager. It was quite funny actually because I ended up doing eleven days there and he called me into his office and said: 'Michael, you've done really well – I just don't think you're quite as good as Rio Ferdinand was at your age.'

That's a moment where you realise what you're competing against when you want to step up to that level; these are the people you'll be compared with and the standards you have to meet. So that was a bit of a wake-up call for me.

The move to Leicester was a bit of a whirlwind. I was going away and my agent old me there was interest but I'd heard it all before so I got on the plane. When I landed I had a load of messages from my agent saying I needed to get back because Leicester wanted to do a deal. I got to the hotel, booked a return flight and two days later I was training with them. That was a huge step up and I felt so lucky to be there.

People talk about players going full circle in their careers and I did do a course with Mark Bonner and still speak to him quite a lot. If I was ever going to go back to Cambridge it would definitely be while Mark's the manager. I want to play as long as I can and when you get older you want to play for a team that means something to you; you want to have passion and you're not doing it for the money. I see myself playing for a club where there's purpose and I want to feel proud to play for them – Cambridge is certainly a club I'd be proud to play for.

34. The Ronaissance
Ron Atkinson

When I went to Cambridge they were down near the bottom of the Fourth Division. I felt if we were going to get better, we had to change the pattern and the style a little bit.

In a very short period of time, I signed three players for £750: Alan Biley, Steve Spriggs and Steve Fallon. They became the backbone of a successful team. My assistant, Paddy Sowden, knew Tom Finney quite well from Sunderland, I think we paid about £9,000 for him. Malcolm Webster came in from Arsenal on the recommendation of Brendon Batson.

The one thing we couldn't ever get hold of was a winger. So subsequently the front players had to switch about and play on the wings. Biley would go out in wide areas and hit great crosses into the box. We were scoring for fun at one stage and all I could think was, 'If I could just get a winger, we could really score some goals!'

I always remember when I was at Cambridge, on a Thursday afternoon John Docherty and I used to ring Bill Shankly up and we'd talk for hours, with Doc listening in. And Shanks said: 'If you get promoted, win the next one as well.' So that was our thinking; it's always been my thinking that whatever league you're in you've got to think you can win it. I did the same at Kettering; we won promotion there and went up and won the league the next year. You've got to believe you can do it.

The year we won the league, I did a swap deal with Keith Bowker going and Jim Hall coming in from Northampton. When I met Jim, he was very up front with me and said bluntly: 'I can't do much; all I can do is score goals.' He worked his socks off, and he was right about scoring goals too.

The camaraderie and the spirit of that team was terrific. We seemed to be celebrating something nearly every week after Christmas. We'd won promotion all but for a miracle, then we had got promotion; then we'd won the championship all but for a miracle, then we had won the championship. There was a celebration going on nearly every weekend.

I have very fond memories of my time at Cambridge.

35. Lockdown season through a lens
Ben Phillips

I worked in the camera shop at Andrew McCulloch's when I was fifteen and learned how to process film. That's when I became fascinated with photography. I used to go up the Abbey taking pictures on my phone, thinking I was pretty good. I printed out one of the South Stand and put it up in the shop and one day someone asked if they could buy it. That really sparked my interest.

When the opportunity came along to combine that passion with my love for Cambridge United by becoming club photographer, I couldn't pass it up. It's a great job but sometimes you have to check your emotions. Like any fan, my first instinct when Cambridge score is to celebrate, but I've still got to make sure I get the shot.

The 2020-21 season was like no other. A season spent almost entirely in lockdown, with no supporters. I found it weird going to empty grounds. I'm so used to capturing the fans and all the atmosphere that goes around a match day, but there was obviously none of that.

I took it for granted after a while that I was getting to see matches when pretty much nobody else was. I had a job to do and just had to get on with it. Then as the season progressed there was this sense something special might be happening, and I just remember thinking: 'Typical Cambridge – we're going to get promoted and nobody is here to see it!'

Watching Wes Hoolahan live in a U's shirt, seeing Paul Mullin scoring for fun – it was a privilege to see it, but you were always wishing that people could be there because the atmosphere would have been amazing.

It was particularly strange going into the game against Grimsby at home. It was such a huge game and I could barely sleep the night before. But again, it was an empty stadium and a very nervous feeling around the place. It was great to be able to capture the celebrations at the end and bring those moments to the fans.

Being involved in that – getting covered in champagne in the changing rooms, helping players get up on the turnstile roof – it was an incredible experience and another reason to love this club.

36. My football education

Danny Granville

Lots of people go to Cambridge University for an education, but I got mine at the football club.

I didn't get offered anything at Tottenham, so when Cambridge were interested my parents thought it'd be great for me. John Beck and Gary Johnson were ahead of their time, with a focus on diet and stuff. My mum and dad came up and they were very impressed by it.

It was tough leaving home at sixteen. To my young mind it felt like I was moving such a long way, going up to Cambridge from London. But moving away and going into digs with sixteen other boys, it makes you grow up. It's like a life education as well as a football one.

I look on it as a great foundation for me, from sixteen to eighteen doing the YTS. It coincided with that great team Cambridge had with Dion Dublin, Steve Claridge, Liam Daish, Alan Kimble – we had so much respect for those first-team players.

I used to clean the boots of Michael Cheetham and Richard Wilkins. It's different nowadays but back then we looked at those players like they were gladiators. I remember, because the ground was so tight at the Abbey, they'd walk out on the pitch and they just looked massive to me.

They were as good as gold with us, too. Obviously they had that authority about them and nobody was lippy or else you'd get put in your place, but they were great with us. You'd get a bit of stick as a young lad but there was a real togetherness, from the youth team all the way up to the first team.

You watched those guys play and you dreamt of getting the opportunity to go and do that yourself, which obviously I did. And there were others, like Micah Hyde and Gary Rowett, who also went on and had good careers.

I think it carries a lot of weight to start your journey in the game at a club like Cambridge United. I learned things there that I wouldn't have if I had started out higher up and I'm grateful for that.

37. Yellow Pages tickertape
Matt King

Cambridge are my local club and I've long had an interest in following their fortunes, albeit my presence at matches has rarely been a good omen for them. My first game was the 2002 LDV Vans final against Blackpool, which set the tone for my track record watching Cambridge.

I've been to around twenty matches and don't recall having seen Cambridge win. I have a close friend who supports the U's and I seem to cause him great pain just by showing up to watch games. I'm actually a West Ham fan and there's a link between the two clubs in that things never run smoothly for either; it's always a journey following them and it certainly keeps it interesting.

One thing the Blackpool game did introduce me to – aside from what would become the familiar feeling of seeing Cambridge lose – was the spectacle of the Yellow Pages tickertape welcome. The most impressive example of it that I was witness to was the play-off final against Torquay (another defeat). I saw people on the train ripping up Yellow Pages with their hands, shoving the torn-off scraps into sandwich bags, and realised that what I'd seen at the Millennium Stadium seven years earlier was not some carefully orchestrated event on an industrial scale, but a homespun spectacle that involved a lot of graft from a handful of people.

It was incredible to see just how much of it there was when it was all thrown into the air as the players came out. It really added to the atmosphere. Wembley was far from full that day but the tickertape blanketed the rows between the seats when it came to rest on the floor. It's something that may well be a thing of the past now, with Google having taken over and the Yellow Pages going out of print.

That's probably a relief to anyone who was ever involved in the clean-up operation afterwards, although if they looked carefully among the tickertape they may have been able to piece together the details of a company who could have helped them with that!

38. The 1977-78 promotion season

CAMBRIDGE SCALE NEW HEIGHTS

Cambridge United fans are in dreamland after the U's secured a second consecutive promotion with a thrilling 2-1 victory over Exeter City.

John Docherty's side recovered from falling a goal behind to former United striker Keith Bowker's goal, with Tom Finney and Steve Fallon turning the game on its head inside the final 20 minutes.

The U's can now look forward to fixtures against the likes of West Ham, Newcastle and Sunderland as the club step up to Division Two for the first time in their history.

It represents a stunning achievement after the mid-season departure of much-loved manager Ron Atkinson, with Docherty taking the wheel and keeping United on course for a second-place finish.

Incredibly, Cambridge lost just once at the Abbey in the league this season, scoring a division-high 49 goals across 23 matches, of which 19 ended in victory for the unstoppable U's.

The triumph over the Grecians sparked scenes of wild celebration on and off the field, with fans given further cause for cheer after rivals Peterborough narrowly missed out on promotion as Preston squeezed ahead of them into third place.

JOHN'S JUST WHAT THE DOC ORDERED

Losing Ron Atkinson to West Brom in January could have knocked United out of their stride, but John Docherty was never going to let that happen.

Even after the disappointment of suffering a 3-1 defeat to

Gillingham in his first game, it was clear Docherty had a firm grip on things and was determined to finish off the job he and Atkinson had started together.

He faces a stern test in the second tier, where United will be a small fish in a big pond.

Pos	Team	Pld	W	D	L	GF	GA	GD	Pts
1	Wrexham	46	23	15	8	78	45	+33	61
2	Cambridge United	46	23	12	11	72	51	+21	58
3	Preston North End	46	20	16	10	63	38	+25	56
4	Peterborough United	46	20	16	10	47	33	+14	56
5	Chester	46	16	22	8	59	56	+3	54
6	Walsall	46	18	17	11	61	50	+11	53
7	Gillingham	46	15	20	11	67	60	+7	50

39. My Football Manager fantasy club
Chris Wood

I've been to the year 2036 and a lot has changed. This is neither a song by Busted nor a wild claim to have invented time travel – this is the world of Football Manager, a fantasy realm where I can take my beloved Cambridge United to places they are never likely to go in real life.

Before I tell you where the U's stand in my simulated reality of the future, I have a confession to make, and I don't feel good about it. My unexpected appointment at Cambridge meant Mark Bonner had to make way when his tenure had barely started. It proved a bitter pill to swallow for Bonz, somehow replaced by an even younger manager. He retired soon after, left to wonder what might have been.

With a good man's professional demise weighing on my conscience, I knew I had to deliver success at the Abbey, which made an 11th-placed finish in my debut season a less than ideal start. Thankfully, brighter days were ahead as a revitalised team spearheaded by the forty-goal Harvey Knibbs stormed to the League Two title.

The third tier could not contain us for long, although the Championship proved a tougher nut to crack. When promotion to the top flight finally arrived in 2027-28, it came a little a too soon and the plucky U's survived only one season among the elite. Undeterred, I rallied the troops for an instant return and they repaid my faith to secure a seat back at the top table at the first attempt.

That paved the way for six seasons (and counting) of Premier League football at The New Abbey Stadium, a 34,000-capacity all-seater affair built in 2029. Not only has it hosted the biggest and best that English football has to offer, but also many of Europe's grandest names amid Champions League campaigns and not one but two trophy-winning Europa League seasons.

My Cambridge career has spanned 5,786 days, encompassing 803 matches, of which 382 have ended in triumph. If anyone should ever have cause to doubt my commitment, I'd point to the fact I've taken just three days' holiday in that time. Maybe Bonz was right to retire when he did – it's a tough gig!

40. Being back where we belong
Josh Coulson

When I used to go and watch Cambridge as a fan with my friends and my dad, it was in the Football League, but when I started playing, we were in the Conference. It wasn't the club I recognised – we're Cambridge United; we're a Football League club.

When we were building up to the first season back in the League, it did feel different. We weren't bothered about when the Conference fixtures came out as we had the Football League fixtures to look forward to, we were in the League Cup, we had the Football League badges on our sleeves. I buy my little boy a Cambridge shirt every year and it's got the Football League badges on. That's more like it.

But we had a job to do – the club was back where it should be, but as a team we had to go and prove ourselves at that level. It didn't feel at all like we weren't good enough and I was just excited to see what we could do. Most of the squad were starting their first season in the League and Plymouth represented a tough first test to see where we were at.

As it turned out, I couldn't have written that day any better; first game back in the League and I managed to scream one in at the Newmarket Road End. It was a corner and up I went. To be honest, on Richard Money's set-plays I was usually just a decoy run for someone else. The ball deflected and fell just right for me – I couldn't have missed. It felt like I kicked it two hundred miles an hour. When it hit the net, I can't even describe the feeling.

I remember Robbie Simpson running with me and I didn't know what to do. It was just sheer joy. The number of times I've had dreams about scoring a goal like that, and then it actually happened. That feeling of running along the front of the Newmarket Road End ... if I had stopped for a moment, I probably could have picked out hundreds of people behind that goal who I know, but it was just a blur of bodies celebrating.

That is right up there in my career highlights. Unlike the play-off final, I just enjoyed that whole day. It was my debut in the Football League, the club was back where it belonged, and I went and scored the winner.

41. My last-minute winner
Scott Rendell

It was a couple of days before the first leg against Stevenage when Gary Brabin told me I wouldn't be starting. I wasn't injured or anything, but he just said he was going with Danny Crow and Lee Phillips. I didn't even get on the pitch, which was a huge disappointment.

There was a shot of me during the game on TV and I looked miserable. The next day at training, Brabs pulled me into the office and tore a strip off me, saying I needed to show more respect and not expect to play every week. He told me he hadn't made a decision for the second leg yet and I needed to train well and prove I deserved to be in the team. I think if you speak to him, he'll claim it was a masterstroke in man-management!

I was told the day before the second leg that I'd be starting. I knew I needed to be on it, so I was raring to go. We felt strongly in that dressing room that we were more than good enough to turn it around. The crowd were a huge factor that day, giving us that edge. I fully believe that's what got us across the line.

We rode our luck at times – Steve Morison missed a gilt-edged chance and Danny Potter made some great saves – but when Robbie Willmott got that deflected goal the whole place erupted and then there was only one team that was going to win it. My equaliser was more relief than anything, just to get level in the tie.

I felt good heading into extra time. It's always been the case with me that if I run for five minutes, my face looks like a beetroot and everyone assumes I'm knackered. But fitness or tiredness did not even come into the equation. I was thinking to myself: 'I could be the hero here.' If there's any striker who tells you they think any differently, they're lying.

Paul Carden decided to have a shot for the first time in a long, long while and when the goalkeeper spilled it, I was there – it may have been offside, but who cares? It's the best feeling you can have, as a striker especially, playing in a play-off semi-final and you've scored the winner. It sounds corny, but it's like something you would dream of as a kid. It was magic. I still remember all of that day practically down to the minute. It's funny how football does that to you.

55

42. It runs in the family
Sam Douglas

My love for the club started as soon as I was born. Dad bought me my first season ticket when I was four and we sat in the Main Stand together. Back then it was just a thing I did, going to watch the team in yellow. Now I have a dog called Dion.

As I got older and spoke to my dad and grandad about the family's connection to the club, I realised how deep it went. My grandad was the vice-chairman back in the 1970s and 80s when the club had managers like Bill Leivers, Ron Atkinson and John Docherty. I started to appreciate just what a big part my family had played in the club, even in the construction of that same Main Stand I sat in as a kid. My dad wrote the programmes back in the day. There's a lot of family history there.

Some of my earliest memories are of going down to the Abbey and watching games with my younger brother, my dad and my uncle. In fact, one of my first memories is going to a game and it was too loud so my mum had to take me home because I was just crying.

I've moved up north now but it's strengthened my link to the club and it's been a focal point for my relationship with my dad, too. There came a time when we stopped going to games; it just happens like that sometimes. But back in 2014 when we reached the play-off final, I got us all together – mc, my dad, my brother and uncle – and we watched Cambridge get promoted at Wembley. It was like I was returning the favour after all those years where my dad took me to games. This was something I could do for him.

The club has always meant a lot to me. When Mallory Knox toured America for the first time, the opening show in San Diego clashed with the FA Cup game against Manchester United. This was a 15,000 sell-out arena show and we were the support act to two other headline bands. I told the tour manager there was no way I was even doing a soundcheck. I couldn't miss the game. He thought I was joking, but soon realised I was completely serious.

There was only one way to resolve it: we got the other two bands – both American, with no clue about football – to watch the game on the tour bus with us. Some of them still follow Cambridge to this day.

43. The kits
James King

I became the proud owner of my first Cambridge United shirt in 1990, when I was fourteen. I bought one every season until my late teens and then eBay appeared. That was a game-changer. Suddenly there was this plethora of shirts and I couldn't help myself; I just kept buying more and more of them.

I used to go home and away back in the late 1980s and into the 90s. Life gets in the way as you grow older and you find you're not able to get to as many games, but some of those shirts can transport you back to a time and place; they hold memories.

Later on, when I was working with Mark Johnson and David Gray who did the programme, I used to pick up the odd one off the club from players who had left or just had a loan spell. The collection grew over time.

Then in 2010 I got laid off, I was out of work and I had to sell off pretty much all of the shirts. I found it a wrench parting with some of them, particularly a few from around the 1970s and 80s, which aren't easy to come by.

I started accumulating them again when I was able to and I'm back up to about 125 now, which is similar to what I had before I had to sell a load. I keep a spreadsheet with them all listed (yes, I know how sad that sounds!). They're worth around £7,000 in total. My favourite one in the whole collection is probably Richard Wilkins' Airtex shirt from a pre-season tour of Sweden in 1992.

All the kits are neatly folded in bags and packed away in boxes, barring a few of the older ones which have earned a promotion to a spot in the wardrobe. The other half isn't a fan of it all, though; she thinks they just get in the way.

I'd happily have a go at designing a kit myself. I have to confess it might not appeal much to the youth, it'd probably be more the older generation that would like my design. I'm a traditionalist; I like the sort of shirt that your average, overweight, forty-something bloke in D block can get away with wearing. We don't all look like Greg Taylor in a football shirt, after all!

44. Luke Chadwick
Tom Champion

There was a whisper that Luke Chadwick was joining Cambridge United. Everyone was familiar with the name as he'd had this amazing career playing for Manchester United. We were sat in the changing room when Richard Money introduced him to us all. He said: 'Luke has reached out to us – he specifically wanted to come and play for Cambridge.' A few of the boys were a bit baffled by it all to be honest.

We were all interested to see how good he was in training and it was clear he still had so much about him. It was obvious he had looked after himself because his fitness levels were excellent. He had moments where you could see he was just a cut above, with his touch, the way he kept the ball and read the play.

It quickly became apparent how much the club meant to him. He grew up watching Cambridge, he still got the new shirt every season, and he knew exactly who all of us were – I found that amazing that he knew who I was. He fitted in straight away; he's such a lovely guy. A lot of the boys were desperate to hear stories from his Man United days and he used to tease us with little snippets, always delivered with this brilliant dry sense of humour he's got.

In the celebrations back at the Abbey after the play-off final win, I saw Luke propped up at the bar and as I worked my way through the crowd towards him, I could see he was holding two bottles of WKD Blue and a few of the boys were having a go at him for it. He just delivered this brilliant one-liner that I'll never forget. He said: 'Yeah, Giggsy and Becks got me on these.' It was such a great line and was typical of his humour.

It's amazing how it worked out for him at Cambridge, for the fairy tale to carry on even after getting promotion at Wembley. He got to play back at Old Trafford in the FA Cup and received a standing ovation wearing Cambridge United colours. That's got to be a rare thing for an opposing player to get that reaction at Old Trafford. It's an unbelievable moment for him to be able to look back on and a fantastic story. I'm glad I was there to be a part of it.

45. The club that shaped my career
Andy Sinton

I was really happy at Cambridge. I left home at a young age and made my debut against Wolves at sixteen. That was where it all began for me and I have some really fond memories of Cambridge. It's a super club.

My first manager was John Docherty. From the age of about fourteen, when I started to come down every weekend on the train, I used to stay at his house. I remember having a trial there and John drove to pick me up.

It was just a real family club. John got on really well with my mum and dad. He was pretty much like a second father, if you like. He saw something in me and wanted to help nurture it.

You obviously need ability but I was also mentally tough, determined, and I was never going to let anything get in my way. I was really dedicated, trained really hard, and had a firm focus on where I wanted to go.

I had a real steeliness, a real desire that I was going to play at the highest level that I could. When I was playing at Cambridge United as a sixteen-year-old, if someone would have said you're going to go on and play for England and go on and play for Spurs, spend the majority of your career playing in the Premier League – it seemed a very far cry from where I was at the time.

As I say, ability is something, but it's not all the bits of the jigsaw, because you need a bit of everything. Careers sometimes just progress on an upward trajectory like mine did, for whatever reason. Sometimes you need a bit of luck, sometimes you get a helping hand.

I made some good mates at Cambridge, some of them I keep in touch with now. There are loads of fantastic memories from a very early age at Cambridge which helped to shape my career.

I'm thankful to the club and grateful for my time there. It's where I met my wife, it's where I got married, it's where my kids were born. It's a fantastic place, I love it. I wish them all the best for the future, whatever it may hold.

46. Steve Claridge
Richard Wilkins

Steve Claridge was different. He had a stall on a market in Portsmouth and he always used to come to away games with loads of bags of fruit; he was always eating fruit. I usually roomed with Steve and I got on really well with him, he just had some quirky rituals. On the first away game he got into the room and took all the bedding off and replaced it with his own, then he just put all the bags of fruit on his bed. He also used to take some of the studs off his boots, which were usually old and worn, and I never understood why.

There's this caricature image of Steve with his socks rolled down, looking scruffy – we used to call him Worzel – but he was, in my opinion, the best footballer among a team of very good players. The system didn't suit him but he adapted to play that system and that's a sign of quality. He was a very intelligent player – very right-footed, too, but that didn't hold him back – and he scored plenty of goals.

I spent a lot of time out injured and when I was watching, I used to love it when Steve got the ball because you knew something was going to happen. He was a little bit like Jack Grealish is now, always likely to get the fans up off their seats.

Him and John Beck didn't always see eye to eye but they respected each other. Becky had a tendency to take people off if they didn't stick to the gameplan. I remember one game when Steve got hauled off at half-time and there was a bit of a kerfuffle between them in the physio's room, but that was just the passion they had. It was a fracas that stemmed from a clash of personalities and it did happen a few times. Steve wanted us to have more freedom to play because teams had sussed us out, but Becky wasn't going to change.

Steve came to my wedding in 1993 and sloped off to go over to Newmarket races and then came back in the evening, spending the whole night doing mad dancing and ending up drenched in sweat. He never used to drink, so after all that he just jumped in his car and drove off down to Portsmouth. He was a character, that's the best way to sum him up; he was always smiling and was just a laugh to be around.

47. Delano Day
Delano Sam-Yorke

I didn't even know I would be playing in that Halifax game until I walked into the changing room and saw my shirt hanging up. I'd been injured. I told the physio I was fine but I didn't realise I was starting until Richard Money read out the team. It was a surprise to me.

I hadn't really been given a run in the team in terms of starting games, even after I scored a couple on the opening day against Halifax. I remember coming into training one day and Richard was like: 'You're going on loan.' I had no say in it, he just told me to pack my bags and go to Lincoln. I was a bit shocked but I just had to go and get some game time and make the most of it.

He ended up calling me back early but I actually didn't want to come back. I was doing well there and I wasn't sure if I had a part to play at Cambridge. I went back and scored in my first game against Kidderminster but it wasn't long before I was out of the team again. That's just how my season went really.

I think Richard saw me as an impact player, someone to bring on if things weren't going right and maybe I could turn it around. I wanted to start and play every game, but you have to get on with it and take your chances when they come.

That second leg against Halifax is a prime example of that. Adam Cunnington was out, we'd brought Sam Smith back from loan to play in the first leg, so we didn't have many options and luckily I was ready to play after an injury of my own. I just did my thing in that game; I expressed myself, I made a nuisance of myself, and the rest is history.

The scenes at the end were crazy, getting lifted above the crowd. I know it's known as Delano Day now and Cambridge fans remind me every year on May 4th. I've watched the highlights quite a few times, I can't lie. It also earned me the opportunity to play at Wembley. My family came to watch, about twenty of them sat near the front row. They are special memories for me, really special memories.

48. A job for life
Ian Darler

The pitch at Cambridge when I arrived in 1979 was like something you'd see on a safari. The ball would bounce up and disappear in a cloud of dust. They had spent hundreds of pounds trying to find out what was wrong with it and I told them for free, which landed me the job as head groundsman – the youngest in the Football League.

The first game of the season was against Leicester and the headline in the paper was nothing to do with the game, but instead declared: 'Leicester directors impressed by pitch.' They made me an offer to work for them but I said, 'I'm sorry gents, but Cambridge have given me a chance to work in professional football and I will stay loyal to them.' I've stuck by that ever since; I'm like the Queen – she signed up to sit on the throne until the day she dies.

I've turned down so many offers over the years and I'm the longest-serving staff member in the club's history. Along the way I've received so many awards and honours but it's not me who has won them, it's all the people who have helped and supported me.

I've worked with around thirty managers, including John Beck, who thought the pitch was too good and wrote me a letter saying it was no longer my responsibility. I asked him what I was going to do with my time and he told me I should go fishing instead. John Docherty stands out as one of the most talented and he treated me like I was his own son. I had a wonderful time when Chris Turner was in charge and Malcolm Webster was there because I never knew from one minute to the next what they were going to do to me.

There have also been tough times and I suffered a serious injury that hugely affected me physically and mentally. I was in such pain that I got to the point of contemplating suicide and I knew I had to seek help. I was told I had PTSD and it has been a six-year journey to recover to where I am now. It made me realise the importance of mental health awareness and being able to talk through things. In fact, the thing I'm most proud of – forget any awards or honours – is being able to help people who are struggling. Having someone to talk to can change the way people think and feel; it can make a huge difference and I will always bang the drum for that.

49. John Taylor
Martin Butler

John Taylor carried a bit of an aura about him because he had been there and done that. We played in the same position so to start with we probably didn't get on as fantastically as we later did, because initially you're just sort of checking each other out to see what the other person is about. Once that initial phase passed – and it soon did – we clicked and formed a really good partnership, with Trevor Benjamin in the mix.

I obviously played with John towards the latter end of his career but you could see he had a bit of everything in his game. His touch was good, he was comfortable on both feet, good in the air, strong, and he could be nasty when he needed to be. The biggest thing about being a striker is scoring goals and he did that all through his career.

In that promotion season in particular, Shaggy really came to the fore. In the big moments when we really needed someone to step up and we were looking around at each other as young lads, he was the one who took responsibility and took all the pressure off our shoulders. That was massive to have somebody of his experience and know-how there to stand up and take on the challenge. It pulled us through that season.

That night at Rochdale still makes the hairs on the back of my neck stand up to think about it. It was meant to be that Shaggy came off the bench and scored the goals to get us promoted. We got a penalty and I didn't fancy it at all, Shaggy said: 'I'll take it.' Of course he stuck it away, then got another one. It's just a great story.

I only have positive things to say about Shaggy. He never looked down on anyone because of what he had achieved and if we ever turned to him for help he'd do whatever he could for us. He was just a really good pro who did things the right way – an all-round good guy, and what higher praise can you give someone than that? Cambridge United and Shaggy just go together perfectly and I'm glad to have played alongside him.

DION IS UNITED'S WEMBLEY HERO

Dion Dublin wrote his name into the history books as he scored the winning goal in the first Wembley play-off final, guiding Cambridge United to a 1-0 victory over Chesterfield.

The young striker rose highest to nod home the only goal of a tense game with just 13 minutes left on the clock. Dublin connected with Chris Leadbitter's corner to head past a stranded Mick Leonard.

That was enough to send John Beck's side into Division Three in front of 26,404 fans on a historic day at the national stadium, capping a stunning five months at the helm for the young boss who took over from Chris Turner in January.

United, who overcame Maidstone over two legs in the play-off semi-finals, finished two points above the Spireites in sixth spot.

It is a remarkable achievement from a side who were languishing in 15th as recently as April, albeit United's stellar run to the FA Cup quarter-finals meant Beck's charges had games in hand.

A fine finish to the campaign sent United into the play-offs as the form team and they delivered the goods when it mattered most in the Wembley sunshine.

DUBLIN'S A STAR IN THE MAKING

Cambridge's entire squad deserve credit for this promotion, but one man in particular will earn

Key players

Dion Dublin (46 appearances, 15 goals): The sky is the limit for this young U's star, who is making Norwich City's decision to let him go appear a very foolish one.

John Taylor (45 appearances, 15 goals): He matched Dublin for goals in the league and was a leading light for United in a glorious season.

Lee Philpott (42 appearances, 5 goals): The provider of so much of the ammunition that allowed Dublin and Taylor to pull the trigger, usually to lethal effect.

special praise after his impressive showing in London.

The U's needed a hero and Dion Dublin was a willing volunteer, putting his head where others may have feared getting hurt.

His beaming smile on the Wembley turf at full-time summed up the emotions of a day that will go down in United's history as one of the very best.

And on the form he has shown, Dublin himself may just carve out a special place of his own in the club's folklore.

Pos	Team	Pld	W	D	L	GF	GA	GD	Pts
1	Exeter City	46	28	5	13	83	48	+35	89
2	Grimsby Town	46	22	13	11	70	47	+23	79
3	Southend United	46	22	9	15	61	48	+13	75
4	Stockport County	46	21	11	14	68	62	+6	74
5	Maidstone United	46	22	7	17	77	61	+16	73
6	Cambridge United	46	21	10	15	76	66	+10	73
7	Chesterfield	46	19	14	13	63	50	+13	71

51. Steve Spriggs
Steve Fallon

It was inspirational to have a player like Steve Spriggs in the team. He was a winner and that rubs off on people, from team-mates to supporters. He wasn't the biggest but he was very aggressive in the way he played the game; he would get up and down the pitch and he could score goals. Spriggy was absolutely pivotal in what the club achieved during his time there.

We were quite different characters – he's from Yorkshire so he's very direct – but we used to room together. Ron Atkinson had a flat overlooking the river and when he got a house, he put the two of us in there. We did everything together and we usually had Alan Biley with us, who was a similar age. It was a great time; we were young and single and we enjoyed every minute of it. Spriggy and I formed a bond over that time and ended up being best man at each other's weddings.

The two of us spent so many seasons at the club and there were times I think I was ahead in appearances, but Spriggy holds that record and there are no hard feelings – although of course it would've been nice to have that for myself! It's much harder now to get that many games at one club so that record will be a hard one to beat.

We actually had a joint testimonial against Manchester United, so we have this long shared history at Cambridge United and it's nice to be remembered at the club in such a positive way by supporters. To see us both in the legends team on the back of the Newmarket Road End is a great honour, it really is. The two of us joined Cambridge as young lads and grew up together at the club, enjoying some of the best years of our lives there. To have spent such a long time there and to have achieved what we did is amazing really.

We don't speak as much as we should these days but we have so many great memories to look back on and I'm glad we had the experiences we did. There are fewer people around now who will have seen us play for Cambridge but whenever I visit the Abbey it brings it all back. That's a nice thing to have and we can both treasure it.

52. Wes Hoolahan

Luke Hannant

The only person I can compare Wes Hoolahan to is Lionel Messi. That's where he gets his nickname from and it's a valid comparison. He is hands down the best footballer I've ever played with or against.

I was in the Academy at Norwich when Wes joined. I used to be a ball boy, so I had a front-row seat to watch all the games. He wasn't particulary well known when he arrived but people quickly saw what a player he was. The magical, almost ridiculous things he would do in games would be what everyone wanted to talk about afterwards.

When I joined Cambridge and heard rumours he was coming in on trial, I just couldn't see it happening. I turned up the first day of pre-season and Wes Hoolahan walked into the changing room. I had to keep my cool – I'm a professional footballer too! – but I was nervous. It was a bit gutting when he didn't sign that first time, but obviously he came back and I'm so glad he did.

Some of the things I've seen him do in training are outrageous. It was a pleasure to watch. He would nutmeg people for fun. He would actually tell me who he was going to nutmeg in training that day and then he would do it with ease. The thing is, you know what he's going to do but you just can't stop him; he does his little drop of the shoulder and he's past you.

Wes will admit he's not the quickest player and never has been, but you don't need to be when you've got snakehips likes him. He runs at people and gets them off balance, sending them three yards in the wrong direction while he just breezes past. He only uses his left foot – his right is literally just for standing on – but I've never seen a player use one foot so well. It's scary.

But it's not just his talent that makes Wes an outstanding player; he's got the same hunger and passion at Cambridge as he had at Norwich, or representing his country. To see that desire and work ethic in someone who has done what he has done is an inspiration to everyone around him.

To come from being a ball boy watching Wes, to playing alongside him and winning promotion with him – that's definitely the biggest achievement in my career so far.

53. Trevor Benjamin
Michael Kyd

Trevor's a gentle giant. He's someone who is great to be around, loves a laugh and a joke, but when it came to football he was deadly serious and determined to make the most of the talents he was given – which were his strength and pace.

He was a nuisance, he was difficult to handle, he had these flailing arms and, above all, he was fearless; he didn't care who he was up against, he would back himself. He had that sort of confidence – not arrogance – that you need, especially as a forward.

Usually when a player first breaks into the team you're not sure what they're about, but with Trevor it was very apparent what he was about – just looking at him you could tell he was going to be strong and make life difficult for defenders.

He worked incredibly hard on improving his game, he trained really hard. Trev was about more than pace and power, for sure; he had a great left foot, he was good in the air, he could pin people, he could turn people. You don't get all the way to the Premier League without having something about you in terms of footballing ability, and Trev just got better and better the more he played.

We were lucky to have Roy McFarland in charge. As a young footballer you need someone who believes in you and shows faith in you, someone who understands you'll have good days and bad days but won't sideline you without explanation or throw you to the wolves. We had a brilliant dressing room under Roy, no cliques, and that definitely helped the likes of myself and Trev when we were starting out.

After Trev got his big move to Leicester – a move he richly deserved – he was still the same old Trev. He never flaunted it, he stayed humble. And he was still the same player, too – I went to watch him play a few times at Leicester and he was still doing his thing.

He's an example to anyone who wants to make the most of what they have, because Trev made sure he got everything out of his talents. He worked hard, he improved himself and he deserved all the success he had. Although I will say this: I was definitely a better footballer than him!

54. The message board

The unofficial Cambridge United forum – affectionately, if a little unimaginatively, known as 'the message board' – represents the largest gathering of U's fans anywhere on the internet. With more than 7,000 members, the online community has grown steadily since its creation in January 2011. It replaced the official forum, which had 1,765 registered accounts.

There are approximately 9,000 threads, the most famed of which – titled 'Transfer Rumours' – extends to over 1,100 pages, featuring more than 16,000 replies. The view count at the time of writing is a staggering 1.7 million. The first rumour in the thread? A post suggesting Connor Jennings might be on United's radar. Still waiting.

At last count there were more than 390,000 posts on the forum, so if you're planning on signing up to read them all, be warned: it's a solid forty-five days' worth of reading if you spent just ten seconds on each post. Though the vast majority of its members share a common passion – namely a love for Cambridge United – the forum lends credence to the notion that football is a game of opinions. You'll be hard pressed to find unanimity on any issue, but won't break sweat in search of discord.

The forum administrator has tales that would enliven this page if he were not bound by a strict code of silence. Rumours abound of players lurking, and who knows if perhaps once a prospective manager did indeed sign up to throw his own name into the discussion about who the next boss ought to be? He won't have liked the response, that's for certain.

A favourite thread comes from the build-up to a match that is best forgotten, with one member posting a link to track the progress of the team coaches up to Harrogate on what proved to be a nightmarish Friday night. The painful progress of those vehicles served as an ominous portent to the many angst-ridden forum users who were frantically refreshing the website and poring over maps to find alternative routes that might somehow be relayed to the drivers.

Strength comes from the shared pain of such experiences and the forum continues to provide a cathartic outlet for thousands of U's fans, through the good and bad.

55. The Habbin
Tom Findlay

The Habbin is populated by those quintessential moany old fans who create no atmosphere. At least, that's what they say. But to me it's the place where all my most precious Cambridge United memories exist. It's where I've always gone to enjoy the game. I've never known any different, and old Habbins die hard!

My first footballing hero was Steve Spriggs. I used to stand right at the bottom of the Habbin, at the front where the stand hugs the touchline, and I can vividly recall just fixating on Steve Spriggs. I was only a kid and he was barely much bigger than me, but he was the most amazing technician. He could curl a football, pick the perfect pass, and for a kid who had never seen anything like that before it was amazing to watch.

That's why I love the Habbin. It's not the stand itself; it's that all my memories and those images of United in my mind's eye are of being stood there, right on the halfway line, watching it all happen. When I go back into my autobiographical memory and I think of Cambridge, I'm transported back to that walk across the common, the click of the turnstiles, the smell of pipe smoke, David Crown scoring on a Tuesday night, Coconuts at full-time (admittedly never often enough).

My support for Cambridge has ebbed and flowed over the years, but at this stage in my life I've really reconnected with the club. During lockdown I watched every week, right up to that last game against Grimsby and those amazing scenes of the players celebrating on the turnstile roof, smoke bombs going off, the fans gathered out in the car park. Those games, the magic of 'Wessi', really sustained me during the worst of that time.

I have enjoyed some incredible experiences during my career in music but I still get a buzz from following Cambridge. I don't mind admitting I felt like that young fan again when I saw that Harrison Dunk was following Groove Armada on Twitter; he's a United cult hero. I'd be insanely excited if I could play in a charity match at the Abbey one day. That might just be better than headlining the main stage at Glastonbury.

56. Cambridge Fans United
Andy Stephen

At the beginning of 2021, I was asked to consider taking over as Chair of CFU and I thought: I like the manager, I quite like the way the club is being run, I admire a lot about the Community Trust, the club are talking about diversity and equality and some of the issues that had previously been overlooked – I just thought there were things I could work on and people I could work with.

It was an exciting time to get involved with CFU because we had young people joining the board with different interests and ideas. Ben Phillips leaves me exhausted; he comes out with one idea after another! Emma Smith is exactly the sort of person we need on our committee; someone who is not afraid to challenge our thinking and present an alternative view. Gina Heath has put so many hours into making the away travel work. Terry Wilby is our secretary, the job nobody wants but he does it extremely well.

What CFU has done since January 2021 is remarkable. The membership has gone up significantly, we've seen the Amber Belles set up, and we're actively supporting different parts of the community and reaching people we've never reached before; we have a wonderful relationship with the mosque, we're working with homeless groups, we're trying to make better provisions for fans with dementia and mobility issues. We want to grow our fan base by welcoming people from all backgrounds and that's where a lot of our focus is now.

We have Dave Matthew-Jones as the CFU-elected director so we have a good level of communication with the club. After I became Chair, I had a long Zoom call with Paul Barry and he told me, 'We may not be at the top of the football pyramid, but we can aspire to be the best for the way we treat our fans.' He understands that without fans there would not be a club. He and the board know CFU will never agree with everything they say and do, but the club is in a much better place and has a far better set of values than in years gone by.

CFU has a philosophy: we believe football clubs are powerful agents within the community and they are a vehicle to improve society. We also believe fans deserve to be taken seriously and treated with respect. I would say to any Cambridge fan who is not a member of CFU: do you want a say in how your club is run, or not?

57. My first match
David Marshall

I don't think anyone can forget their first football match. Some of the details may fade over time, but certain things stick with you. In my case, a chance encounter with a Cambridge legend made sure of that.

My first game was back in 1994. It's not the kind of game you would remember unless it was your first, or you happened to meet your hero. It was in the Auto Windscreens Shield against Northampton Town on a cold October school night. It might not sound like much to get excited about but I didn't care because this was the first time my dad had ever taken me to a football match.

I remember the sound of the crowd from the Newmarket Road End and the tannoy announcements from the Main Stand. There was a real buzz of excitement for the match to start.

But my highlight of the evening had nothing to do with what happened on the pitch; it came after I heard someone next to me talking to their friend, excitedly declaring: 'Dion's over there.' I looked around and I could see Dion Dublin trying to keep a low profile, tucked away in the top corner of the Main Stand. At that moment I had one mission in life – I had to get his autograph.

I didn't waste any time, because what if Dion had left before I could get to him? My chance would be gone forever. I grabbed a pen from my dad and ran up the stand before anyone else could get there.

First in the queue, I was quickly surrounded by other children eager to get the former Manchester United striker's signature. But I was first and that was all that mattered. I returned to my seat bursting with pride that I had got Dion's autograph to show my friends the next day.

The scoreline was one to forget, even though I haven't managed to, as the Cobblers ran out 3-1 winners, but for me it was the start of a wonderful journey following this football club and a night I will never forget.

58. Roy McFarland
Andy Duncan

When I came on loan to Cambridge from Manchester United and met Roy for the first time, there was an immediate sense that what you were getting was a genuine guy. He was very honest and frank and that approach creates a mutual respect. But what Roy really excelled in was building a team spirit.

He had played at the highest level but that in itself doesn't guarantee you'll make a good manager, and he put the work in. The camaraderie he had with all the players is something that stands out. I think that's why he got such good performances and good results; he had everybody on board. Obviously there were certain players who weren't playing some weeks, but nobody sulked. He had everybody as a tight-knit group.

He never used to let the players go straight after training; you always had to wait around to see if he wanted to talk to us and he often did. Sometimes Roy would come in with nothing much to say but he would get us having a singsong or whatever. His style of management was definitely about creating that togetherness.

The saddest day of my time at Cambridge United was when Roy got the sack. I remember it quite clearly. We were struggling at a higher level and going to away games and, quite frankly, being outclassed. It wasn't going according to plan but I for one didn't see it coming at all.

The way Roy dealt with it summed him up. Roy wanted to tell us the news himself and it was a very emotional dressing room. It's the way he said things; he had a touch of class. He told us: 'You're my boys.' I remember looking around the dressing room and some of the boys were welling up. He said it from the heart.

You maybe don't fully appreciate what you've got until it's gone sometimes. His popularity in the dressing room, his charisma, his man-management, the way he dealt with situations – everybody wanted to play for him. It even went beyond the dressing room; everyone at the club enjoyed their time with Roy.

59. The rivalry
Barry Fry

In my first press conference as Peterborough manager, I made a big mistake. A journalist asked me about Cambridge and I said: 'I love Cambridge. I've got a great relationship with some of the people there.' Well, that was nearly my job gone on day one! The fans wanted me out. I had no idea the level of hatred between the two clubs.

I soon found out. The passion of the supporters is amazing. Every time we got the fixture list, the first ones you'd look for were Cambridge home and away. You could lose all your other games, as long as you didn't lose those two you were alright.

The players would get themselves up for those games as well, not just the fans. There's an extra edge to it. I think the beauty of it is, even with the fierce rivalry and the passion and commitment of the fans, after the game – and I'm talking about club officials here – you'd all be mates, having a drink together. I'm not sure the same applies to the supporters!

I know what they sing about me at the Abbey, but that's all part of the fun of football. I think Cambridge fans hated me before I even became Posh manager, for the simple reason that when I was at Birmingham I nicked Steve Claridge and Liam Daish off them. That was just another reason to hate me when I went to Posh. I'm a football fan at heart and I understand it.

We've done some deals over the years, taking players from Cambridge. I know it's never a popular one. We took Scott Rendell and that ruffled a few feathers. I didn't realise he had said on TV he wouldn't be leaving, so when he turned up down the road at your enemies someone had to get the blame, and it's usually me.

To be honest, I'm happy to see Cambridge do well. When they got promoted, I sent Mark Bonner a message of congratulations – 'Miracle Man' I called him; it's incredible what he achieved. He did it his way. He's a very cool, calm and collected guy and I was delighted for him.

I really want the derby to be a regular fixture again; that would be good for both clubs and the fans. The sooner that happens the better.

60. The 1990-91 promotion season

BRILLIANT BECK DELIVERS TITLE

John Beck steered Cambridge to the Division Three title with a richly deserved 2-0 final-day win over Swansea at the Abbey.

First-half goals from Steve Claridge and Lee Philpott ensured United held up their end of the bargain as fellow title hopefuls Southend slipped up against Brentford, meaning the U's finished top of the pile.

Fans invaded the pitch at full-time to rejoice with the jubilant players as United head for Division Two after a second consecutive promotion under the brilliant Beck.

In another season involving a run to the FA Cup quarter-finals, where this time defeat to top-flight Arsenal ended hopes of a trip to Wembley, the U's won few admirers from outside of Cambridge.

Beck's rigid long-ball tactics have drawn criticism from many quarters, though jealousy at his incredible success may well be a motivating factor for his detractors.

RESULTS JUSTIFY BECK'S METHODS

Cambridge United do not play a style of football aimed at pleasing the neutral, and it certainly does little to raise the spirits of their beaten and battered opponents; what dogmatic boss John Beck has at the forefront of his mind is results.

Key players

Dion Dublin (46 appearances, 16 goals): Another fine campaign from the forward as his reputation continues to blossom.

Richard Wilkins (41 appearances, 3 goals): His long throw is a weapon, but the classy midfielder offers so much more than that.

John Taylor (40 appearances, 14 goals): Like strike partner Dublin, he is a beneficiary of United's direct approach and he really makes it count.

When you look at what he has achieved in his one and a half seasons at the helm – a quick reminder that he has masterminded two promotions and two runs to the FA Cup quarter-finals – you see very quickly how productive his win-at-all-costs mentality is.

And his players, though capable of playing a more attractive brand of football, are happy (for the most part!) to follow their young manager's instructions to the letter. That's a winning combination: a man with a plan, and a team who will back him to the hilt.

Pos	Team	Pld	W	D	L	GF	GA	GD	Pts
1	Cambridge United	46	25	11	10	75	45	+30	86
2	Southend United	46	26	7	13	67	51	+16	85
3	Grimsby Town	46	24	11	11	66	34	+32	83
4	Bolton Wanderers	46	24	11	11	64	50	+14	83
5	Tranmere Rovers	46	23	9	14	64	46	+18	78
6	Brentford	46	21	13	12	59	47	+12	76
7	Bury	46	20	13	13	67	56	+11	73

61. Harrison Dunk
Mark Bonner

Resilient. Intelligent. Affable. They are three words to describe Harrison Dunk, but there's so much more to say about him.

It's clear the type of culture we want to build at Cambridge and Harrison typifies that; he's a role model. At heart he's just a really sound human being with good morals and consistent behaviours. He's a brilliant character and a good influence.

He's had competition with Jack Iredale and Jack's comment to me was: 'How can I get annoyed with Harrison? He's the nicest guy in the world!' And that sums him up. It doesn't mean he's not competitive, it doesn't mean he doesn't drive standards and deliver at a high level, it just means he does those things with respect.

There have been a few versions of Harrison during his ten years with the club. When he first signed he was a flying left-winger and that made him an instant attraction to our supporters. People want to be up off their seats in anticipation and he provided that. Over the years his game has evolved, he's improved on the defensive side and he's more versatile. He's got really good game intelligence and thinks deeply about the game.

Harrison has been through so much with the club and your love for someone grows when it's been tough and you've endured it together. That experience makes the good times even sweeter. That's why you need people like Harrison.

It was great to see him get his testimonial, which was so richly deserved for someone who has served this club brilliantly. You don't last ten years at the same club, through multiple managers, without having the right qualities. He's had times where he's been out of the side or had injury setbacks and Harrison always finds himself back in the team. That tells you not only about his ability, but also about his character.

It's that kind of spirit you want in your dressing room and he exudes those qualities whether he's in the team or not, which tells you all you need to know about Harrison.

62. Paul Barry
Renford Sargent

Paul Barry has been the most important person to Cambridge United in the last twenty years. You cannot overstate Paul's importance to the club, especially from a financial standpoint. Without Paul's backing, this club would not exist – there is absolutely no doubt about that. He's put more money into this club than anyone, by a long way.

In the early days, Paul poured a lot of money into the club without much involvement in the way it was run. We've now assembled a very good board here – there are no egos – and Paul is more involved than he has ever been. He really does understand the football business; he can have conversations with Mark Bonner and Ben Strang and offer valuable input on transfers and sell-ons and the like.

Paul and I actually joined the board on the same day. We had things in common as we're both in the travel industry; Paul was one of the first people to do online travel from the States to Europe and he was very successful at that. But what we spoke about most was the U's – that's what we had both grown up with.

People like Paul and I, and in fact across the whole board now, we live it; we kick every ball. We've pretty much always been on the same wavelength in terms of the people we want to bring in and the direction we want the club to go in.

There have been times when he's had doubts, not that he's ever wanted to walk away – the club is such a huge part of his life, and probably has become more so over the years. There was a significant turning point where as a board we persuaded shareholders that it was best for Paul to be the sole owner of the club. He has been able to bring in two new investors from the States, and nobody else could have attracted investment at that level.

When we got promoted to League One, we both said how much more it meant to us because of the people we had around at the club to share it with. People like Mark Bonner and Harrison Dunk; great ambassadors for the football club. Paul is not the most emotional or expressive person but there is no question the club means a great deal to him.

63. Under the Abbey Stand podcast

Under The Abbey Stand was conceived in The Dobblers Inn off Mill Road around Christmas in 2017, with Julian Roberts and Tom Walker its proud parents. The podcast was made to fill a gap left by the absence of a fanzine; a modern alternative intended to give supporters an independent platform to air their views.

The duo roped in Jack Swindlehurst to host and put out the first episode of UTAS the week after Shaun Derry had been sacked and Harrison Dunk had scored a last-minute winner at Chesterfield under Joe Dunne. As much as the club's fortunes have transformed since then, so too has the pod. The UTAS crew produce a fanzine and run a regularly updated website, while two new members, Jordan Worland and Owen Kiernan, have been added to the team. Speaking of which, here's a little more about each:

Julian: Responsible for editing the fanzine, unfairly named the pod happy clapper. Adores Tom Champion.

Jordan: Habbinite, leader of the pod's old guard, and passionate only when talking about Wes Hoolahan.

Owen: The brilliant website editor, obsessed with Lionel Perez and Andy Dallas. Avid kit collector.

Tom: Never missed an episode, some might call him the pessimist of the pod. Claims to have three separate autographs from Wes.

Jack: The pod's outsider hails from Carlisle but has adopted the real United as his team. Owner of a wonderfully deep voice, which is one of reason.

The team – who have welcomed special guests including Greg Taylor and Max Rushden, and whose peak audience figures have ventured into four-figure territory – are always on the lookout for more United fans to get involved with the podcast, website or fanzine as they seek to keep building the UTAS brand from its humble beginnings in a Cambridge boozer.

64. The loanee legend
Kwesi Appiah

As soon as I stepped in the door at Cambridge, the way the guys took me in was just amazing. I just hit it off from day one, not only with the players and staff but with the fans and the club as a whole. I don't know what it was, whether it was my personality or the way I interacted with the fans, but they were in my corner and we had this great bond.

I just felt comfortable at Cambridge and the belief the manager had made me want to go out there and fight for the team as if it was my team; I'm not a loan signing, I'm a permanent signing, this is my team, these are my colleagues, these are my brothers out on the pitch and we're going to do well together. I think people will have seen that in how I played; I just gave everything.

My relationship with Richard Money was the best I've had with any manager. He was almost like an additional parent. He had such belief in me and that gave me the confidence to do what I knew I could do on the pitch, and you guys saw that with my performances at Cambridge. I was at a stage where maybe I wasn't ready to be playing regularly in the Championship, but dropping down to the Conference I think Richard realised I was better than that level, so he expected me to light it up. Thankfully, we managed to produce the goods.

I didn't have the pressures that some of the players had because I was just starting out my journey in professional football, so for me it was just a case of going out there and enjoying myself, and that drew the fans towards me because I was getting people up off their seats and scoring goals. I played my game and they loved me for what I did, and I have so much respect and fondness for this club – I don't even think the fans would understand.

Even now I'm always getting messages on Twitter from Cambridge fans asking when I'm signing, and I love it to be honest. Conversations have happened and it's something I've always wanted to do, but the stars have never quite aligned. It would be a fairy tale for me to come back and everyone would be buzzing about it, but I think you have to be careful because the club is in a different place, I'm in a different place. But you never know what the future holds.

65. Steve Fallon
Steve Spriggs

Steve was a big, raw centre-half who used to think he could play a bit, like all centre-halves do. Fal would tell you he was the best five-a-side player in the world! Every now and then you had to tell him just to do his stuff and that's enough. Dave Stringer was on at him all the time; Fal would go up for corners and when the ball was pinging about he'd stay up there while Dave was tearing his hair out telling him to get back where he should be.

We're quite different, me and Fal; I'm from Yorkshire so what you see is what you get and if I've got something to say I'll say it. Fal's not like that; he's quieter and more laid-back. You can't imagine how many times Fal's had to tell me off for swearing. Sometimes he daren't phone me these days because I might end up going off on one.

We never clashed though. I knew he would've wanted the appearance record at Cambridge but we were such good mates that he would never have let it interfere with what we had personally. He did as much as I did at that club, he was just unfortunate to have his knee injury or else he would've sailed past me.

We had a very good team at Cambridge for many years and we competed against some big clubs; we weren't just making up the numbers in Division Two. Fal was a big part of that and I suppose like a few of us – myself included – he could've gone on to a bigger club.

When we were flying high in the Second Division I think there was some interest in Fal from Tottenham, and if Fal had pushed for it that move might have happened. But he's not like that. John Docherty would've called him in to his office and said, 'Tottenham have offered us this much for you – we haven't accepted it' and Fal would've said, 'Okay' and walked out. Honestly, he wouldn't have forced it at all; that's just how he is.

He decided to go down the coaching and management route after he'd finished playing and the job he did at Histon was unbelievable. I'm not sure he gets enough recognition for what he did there, because it was an incredible job.

66. Alan Biley

Graham 'Willie' Watson

Alan Biley had the nickname Rod Stewart because of his hair, but I used to call him Shirley Temple. He was a nice kid. He arrived around the same time as Steve Spriggs and Steve Fallon, and they really helped push the team on. It was already a very good side with the players we had, but Biley definitely added another dimension to it.

He absolutely bounced around the place. He was so quick, which suited the way I played. I loved to put a near-post ball in and Biley was that sharp he would usually get on the end of it. I'd say he would stick about one in five in the back of the net, which made me look good. It's nice because every time I see him down at Cambridge he'll say: 'Here's the man that made me!' It's a load of bull of course, but it's still nice to hear.

I wouldn't say Alan was the best footballer in the world but he was so eager. He would get in behind defenders, like Raheem Sterling does now at Manchester City, and I think supporters love to see it when players do that. It's exciting. If you put the ball at his feet one-on-one with anyone, you'd always fancy his chances.

He actually broke his leg in a game at Charlton early on in his Cambridge career and he was out for about six months, so he did well to come back from that. It's a good job he did; he was an important part of that team.

It was an exciting team under Ron Atkinson, the Abbey was a fortress and nobody liked coming to play against us. Clubs like Sheffield Wednesday, big clubs, we would turn them all over. Biley was a big part of that and it was no surprise when he got his move to Derby, and he even had a spell at Everton. He scored plenty at Portsmouth but I fancied him to score goals wherever he went.

If you put the ball in the box for Biley, he'd get on the end of it – whether he was going with his feet or his head. He wasn't tremendously tall but he was fabulous in the air, he had an amazing spring on him – I think he should have been a high jumper.

67. Harrison Dunk's United XI

Goalkeeper – Will Norris: He arrived as this little beanpole and became a man. He was a great goalkeeper and a really good guy to have around the dressing room.

Left-back – Greg Taylor: He's such a class guy and he's turned into a real leader. He's a lot better on the ball than people realise and he rarely makes mistakes.

Right-back – Kyle Knoyle: Strong, quick and so good on the ball, Knoyley was just an all-round great right-back. He was so confident in possession and he had a great delivery on him.

Centre-back – Josh Coulson: Mr. Cambridge has to go in. He's not only a class guy but a really good player. He was so solid at the back and he'd be my pick for captain as well.

Centre-back – Leon Legge: Leggey would head a brick wall, he was absolutely dominant. You want a guy like him in your team; a real commanding figure. He scored a few goals too.

Centre-midfield – Paul Digby: This was between Diggers and Tom Champion, but Diggers runs all day and he breaks up everything. Also, I still have to face him in training!

Centre-midfield – Ryan Ledson: He was fresh from Academy football, but you could see his talent straight away. He could do everything with the ball.

Centre-midfield – Luke Berry: Bez is one of the most naturally gifted players I've ever played with. He scored goals and he won every header despite being small – that was his party trick.

Attacking midfield – Wes Hoolahan: You haven't seen the half of it. People are scared to go near him or you'll get nutmegged. He sees passes nobody else does. He's just a joy to watch.

Striker – Paul Mullin: On the basis of that promotion season, I can't leave Mulls out. He just put away every chance that came his way. I used to room with him too.

Striker – Barry Corr: All I had to do was put the ball in the box and Baz would get on the end of it. Off the pitch he was the nicest guy, but on it he turned into a bit of an animal.

Manager – Mark Bonner: You wouldn't find anyone with a bad word to say about Bonz, and yet he's not too nice. You respect him and you wouldn't want to cross him.

U'S PROMOTION IS TAYLOR-MADE

John Taylor came off the bench to fire Cambridge to promotion with a 2-0 win at Rochdale.

The beloved striker stirred a tense match into life after his late introduction, netting a penalty and heading home a second as the U's capitalised on Scunthorpe's loss at Halifax to ensure a top-three spot.

It had threatened to be a frustrating night at Spotland, with lowly Rochdale determined not to be the unwilling hosts of a promotion party.

But Roy McFarland turned to a wise old head from the bench, with Taylor's arrival lifting the mood of his team-mates and the expectant travelling fans.

He converted from the spot after Trevor Benjamin had been fouled, putting the U's within touching distance of the third tier.

And the man lovingly known as 'Shaggy' had not finished there. With two minutes remaining, he rose to meet Alex Russell's free-kick with a fine header to spark wild scenes in the away end.

The result sent United top with three games left, having surrendered first place following a 1-1 draw with rivals Peterborough last time out.

SUPER-SUB SHAGGY'S LEGEND GROWS

John Taylor was an anxious observer for 82 minutes at Rochdale, but the striker who

Key players

Martin Butler (46 appearances, 17 goals): A goalscoring output to match his incredible work rate, Butler's all-action displays make him a shining example.

John Taylor (40 appearances, 17 goals): Another chapter added to Taylor's incredible story in amber and black. The legend grows.

Paul Wanless (45 appearances, 8 goals): A fine campaign from the skipper, whose contribution to this season's success cannot be overstated.

this season became Cambridge's record goalscorer knows how to make an impact.

It has been a joy to see this Abbey legend in action this season, with Taylor overtaking Alan Biley as the club's most prolific marksman in the Football League.

Shaggy has drawn upon his vast experience to marshal an exciting forward line that includes the bustling Trevor Benjamin and the relentless Martin Butler.

His two-goal cameo was the perfect way for Roy McFarland's men to seal promotion.

Pos	Team	Pld	W	D	L	GF	GA	GD	Pts
1	Brentford	46	26	7	13	79	56	+23	85
2	Cambridge United	46	23	12	11	78	48	+30	81
3	Cardiff City	46	22	14	10	60	39	+21	80
4	Scunthorpe United	46	22	8	16	69	58	+11	74
5	Rotherham United	46	20	13	13	79	61	+18	73
6	Leyton Orient	46	19	15	12	68	59	+9	72
7	Swansea City	46	19	14	13	56	48	+8	71

69. The Community Trust

Graham Daniels

The Community Trust is Cambridge United's primary way of impacting upon and enriching the community independently of playing football. The work of the Trust is broken down into four key areas: community engagement, wellbeing, inclusion, and education. Through that the Trust has positively impacted the lives of many thousands of people of all ages across our community since it was set up in 2011, and continues to do so.

One area the Trust has excelled in is mental health and we were ahead of the curve in appointing a Mental Health Officer. We started a campaign called Mind Your Head, with Liam O'Neil as our ambassador, and filmed a number of players giving testimony on the subject of mental health and dealing with issues. That campaign was recognised by the EFL, who gave us the Community Project of the Year Award, and we are very proud of that. It ties in with the fact Godric Smith is Chair of the Duke of Cambridge's mental health charity and it shows how deep our commitment is in that area.

When you look at the work Phil Mullen has done on inclusion, particularly with mentally and physically disabled people in our ward, that's another area in which the Trust has had an outstanding impact and made a real difference. We've also had the AstraZeneca Science in Schools project, which has enormous reach with so many headteachers wanting in on it.

We also saw the incredible power of the Trust when the pandemic hit and we went all hands on deck, with people right across the club helping out – joining Zoom calls, getting on the phone, delivering meals; it was exhilarating to see people like Mark Bonner and Matt Walker getting involved with that and it underlines the pride the club has in the Trust.

There is a systemic belief that part of being a football club is that you have an unprecedented opportunity to bring a community together. It gives you an amazing opportunity to build something that is inclusive of people of all backgrounds and all ages. There is such a firm belief in the fundamental values of the Trust and the work it does and that's what I'm most proud of; I think it's something we can all be proud of. In the Trust, we have something truly special and it's a beautiful thing.

70. Paul Mullin's record-breaking season

Paul Mullin's Football League goals, 2020-21 season:		
12th September, 2020	Carlisle United (H)	⚽
19th September, 2020	Morecambe (A)	⚽ ⚽ ⚽
10th October, 2020	Newport County (H)	⚽ ⚽
17th October, 2020	Scunthorpe United (A)	⚽ ⚽
20th October, 2020	Port Vale (H)	⚽ ⚽ ⚽
27th October, 2020	Walsall (A)	⚽
24th November, 2020	Cheltenham Town (A)	⚽
5th December, 2020	Oldham Athletic (H)	⚽
15th December, 2020	Colchester United (H)	⚽ ⚽
26th December, 2020	Leyton Orient (H)	⚽
2nd January, 2021	Grimsby Town (A)	⚽
6th February, 2021	Barrow (A)	⚽
9th February, 2021	Salford City (A)	⚽
20th February, 2021	Mansfield Town (H)	⚽ ⚽
6th March, 2021	Walsall (H)	⚽
13th March, 2021	Oldham Athletic (A)	⚽
27th March, 2021	Carlisle United (A)	⚽
2nd April, 2021	Morecambe (H)	⚽ ⚽
5th April, 2021	Tranmere Rovers (A)	⚽
20th April, 2021	Leyton Orient (A)	⚽
30th April, 2021	Harrogate Town (A)	⚽ ⚽
8th May, 2021	Grimsby Town (H)	⚽
Total: 32		
⚽ ⚽		

71. Liam Daish

Danny O'Shea

The first thing that springs to mind with Liam is the frown on his forehead – he was always sulking! I played plenty of games alongside Liam, we've had plenty of beers together and we enjoyed a lot of success together at Cambridge as well.

He was a good footballer, an international footballer in the end, which came as no surprise to me. He had a good left foot on him, he was strong and he had a winning mentality. He could play when he needed to; drop his shoulder and get out of trouble. He was the perfect fit for Cambridge at that time and he was a great player to have in that team and a big voice in the dressing room.

John Beck had this thing he used to say to me because I always wanted to play a little bit more than he wanted me to. He'd say: 'Take your Arsenal hat off, Danny.' It was a regular thing; he'd say it often in training. Anyway, we did Secret Santa in my first Christmas there and when I unwrapped mine it was an Arsenal hat. Turns out Liam had got it for me.

It wasn't me who got Liam's gift, but he was minus a kidney so somebody thought it'd be a good idea to get him another one!

I actually got to play in the Wembley play-off final because Liam was suspended. It's swings and roundabouts really; I'd had to sit on the bench for the semi-final games against Maidstone and it was a huge opportunity for me but obviously a big one for Liam to miss out on. He was very supportive though and there was always a lot of competition in that centre-half position – when Mick Heathcote came you had four going for two spots, with Liam, myself and Phil Chapple also in the reckoning.

Becky used to tell us we'd look back on our days at Cambridge and realise we had the time of our lives, and he was right. We were so close to getting into the Premier League and it was a really special time to play for that club. Everything we did, we did together. We didn't have a huge squad and we had a great bond together. Having people like Daishy there made it what it was and he was one of quite a few from that team who went on to have really strong careers. I've got a lot of respect for him and I'm glad to see he's still in the game now.

72. Johnno bingo

Mark Johnson is the voice of Cambridge United commentaries on BBC Radio Cambridgeshire, delivering incisive, vivid and frequently witty updates to a captive audience.

As linguistically creative and articulate as Johnno may be, he is not averse to relying on some of his own well-worn phrases to describe the action. Next time you tune in, why not play a game of Johnno bingo using the card below:

BINGO

Capricious breeze	Back on defensive duty	A minimum thereof	Agricultural
Thwacked	Episcopal purple	Bowled out in an instant	Cleared their lines
Marauds forward	Eschews	Posthumous appeal for a free-kick	With aplomb
We're now in the fourth of the three added minutes	Hacked away	Of that ilk	Ran into a crowd scene

73. It's like a family
Paul Wanless

Cambridge United is like a family to me; I've never felt more at home than I did at that football club. You spend eight years somewhere, you fall in love with the place. I fell in love with the fans and they loved me.

I go back now and there are just so many memories. I was there when we got promoted against Grimsby and when we left we walked across the common, and I remember training over there on a winter's day in the snow. These memories just come flooding back to you. Everything about the club was lovely and special.

Then there's the games that stick in your mind and the moments you'll never forget – winning promotion at Rochdale, the LDV Vans final. We had the cup runs: going to Hillsborough, that amazing game at Nottingham Forest when we came back from 3-0 down, beating Watford.

They were amazing times and it's given me some really special memories that will live with me for the rest of my days. There are actually too many to be able to pick a favourite.

Still to this day I go back to the club and it puts a smile on my face. There's one really special moment I had when I took my son to the Abbey and he saw the Wanless Bar and photos of me – he couldn't believe it. That was a really proud moment. It makes me think that maybe I did alright at that club, to still be remembered.

When they did the fans vote for which names to have on the back of the shirts painted on the Newmarket Road End and my name was on there, that was another proud moment for me. It's special for me and for my family.

There was one time I went back and I had my daughter Emily with me, and the steward said: 'That's the best midfielder ever to wear our shirt.'
And Emily said: 'So you were alright were you, dad?'
I guess I wasn't too bad.

74. The award-winning bacon butties

Ben Riley-Smith

I fell for Cambridge United when I was eleven. My dad, on something of a whim, went out and bought season tickets for us three brothers and himself. Up to then I had been an Arsenal fan, inherited from my older brother. That was an affection grown from afar, through TV highlights and the pages of Match magazine. This was something else entirely.

It was the 1998-99 season, a glorious time to be a U. Trevor Benjamin and Martin Butler up front, Andy Duncan clearing everything at the back. Roy McFarland barking instructions. The exhilaration of attending football matches when a young lad is hard to capture. Maybe Nick Hornby came closest in Fever Pitch, describing the outpouring of adult emotion in a stadium being unlike anything else in normal life. We could walk to the Abbey from home and with each few minutes the excitement would ramp up. First spotting others in yellow and black scarfs, then hearing the chants from the terrace, before turning a corner and seeing the floodlights loom.

Every supporter of a club gets that. But what others cannot boast is one of the consistent delights of Abbey matches – the bacon butties. Everyone would have their own half-time strategy for getting theirs. I was never one for skipping the final minutes of the first half, so would trade the longer queues to wait for the whistle. In my mind I picture a Tuesday evening game in the pouring rain, reaching out for a piping hot butty soon to be slathered in ketchup and a cup of Bovril with gloved hands. Probably 1-0 down. Heaven.

It was not just local boasting either. On at least one occasion Colman's Football Food Guide put us top of football stadiums across the UK for the quality of bacon butty served up. It was a title to cling to during the hard times. The 98-99 promotion season was a mirage for a young U's fan. The next decade would be a slide south, with plenty of humiliation along the way.

There was the season the away stand was just a stretch of grass and a fence when we ran out of money for the redevelopment. The slump into the Conference. Administration. But that is the joy of lower league football. So rarely are you in the spotlight that when success comes your way – even just a bacon butty trophy – it tastes all the sweeter.

75. Carol Looker – forever a U

Dave Matthew-Jones

Walking past the Cut Throat Lane turnstiles on a match day or travelling on the away travel coach can never be the same again. Gone is the familiar and welcome sight of Carol Looker selling raffle tickets or 50/50 tickets. She was a master of selling tickets. However hard you tried to avoid buying one, she would lure you in with a warm persistence that few could resist.

Carol's love affair with Cambridge United began when she attended her first match at the Abbey Stadium more than fifty years ago. I first met Carol when she ran the Away Travel Race Nights. They were organised so that a collective group could afford to sponsor a player and support the club.

She did so much for United over the years. When the club was on its knees, she was there to help out in the club shop or ticket office. She would always do whatever was needed to help support the club and players she loved.

How many supporters below the age of thirty-five have made their away match travel arrangements through Carol? How many younger ones were looked after by her? Without Carol they would not have been able to travel on their own to matches.

The players she sponsored and those she supported from the terraces all loved her and she never let them down with her loyal and unwavering support. She never criticised anyone who wore the black and amber of her beloved Cambridge United.

Football clubs need supporters like Carol; individuals who give everything to the cause, never questioning and only supporting. I am sure Carol will be waiting for the arrival of every Cambridge United supporter at the gates of heaven to offer us a friendly welcome and to ask if we want 'one ticket for fifty pence or three for a pound.'

Rest in peace, Carol.

76. The Manchester United games
Tom Elliott

I won't lie, my first thought when we got Manchester United in the FA Cup was: 'Whose shirt can I get after the game?' After that draw was made, my phone was just going off non-stop with people saying: 'You've got Man United!' It was great to have beaten Luton in the third round because I used to love our battles against them, and then to get Man United just rubbed it in their faces.

We didn't know what sort of team they were going to name, but we were hoping they put the big boys out. The overriding feeling was one of excitement; we just wanted to make the most of it and enjoy it. The whole build-up was intense and we were under the national spotlight, with everyone talking about Cambridge United, so you felt like a hero even before the game.

The home game was almost like a dream. I can remember the noise of the crowd, particularly whenever Ryan Donaldson got the ball – he was having one of his best games and every time he got possession the volume just went up a notch. The whole experience was surreal, from seeing people like Falcao and Di Maria on their team sheet, to the atmosphere – it just went by in a blur and suddenly the final whistle went and we had got a 0-0 draw.

I remember the game up at Old Trafford more clearly. That stadium is like the Colosseum; when you're on that pitch looking up at the stands, it's huge. Before kick-off, I asked Robin van Persie if I could have his shirt at the end of the game. It was about sixty seconds later I was through on goal. I still watch it back now and it annoys the life out of me – my left foot slipped as I went to place it so I was over-stretching and hit the post. That would have been one of the best moments of my life if I had scored against David de Gea at Old Trafford.

I still enjoyed the game, playing against basically their strongest team and they were so good. I did enjoy the experience of seeing them play. Van Persie got subbed off in the second half and I thought there was no way he'll remember me. But – and this is probably one of the nicest things that's happened to me in football – after the game he came to the dressing room and gave his shirt to the kitman to give to me. He showed he was a gentleman. I put the shirt straight on; I was buzzing.

77. My second chance
Brendon Batson

It was a rude awakening coming from Arsenal to join Cambridge United. I must admit it took me a little time to adjust. I was still living in London and travelling up to Cambridge. I got married in the June, moved up to Cambridge, and it was this sudden realisation that, having been at a First Division club and being a potential top-tier player, I was going to be plying my trade in the Fourth Division.

I knew nothing about Cambridge apart from the fact it was a university city, and that was it. I didn't care what division they were in at the time and I just wanted to be in somebody's first team.

They told me about the situation and them being a new club to the Football League. Cambridge were struggling and they thought maybe I could help them get out of a bit of trouble. I was flattered by it all really and I was just very happy to know that someone wanted me to play for them.

I thought, well, there's only one way I can go if I want to have a career in the game, and that's up. I really worked on my fitness, that's one of the things Ron Atkinson encouraged. I was always quick but I knew I used to struggle on distance and stuff like that, and Ron used to challenge me.

He really helped me to change my attitude, no question. This was serious now; this was my career and I had to do something. I just wanted to play in a higher division. I thought, if I get a chance, I wanted one chance to play in the top flight again and then we'll see what happens, and it was Cambridge that gave me that chance, without doubt.

I've lived all over the place and I've always said I'm a bit of a nomad. I was born in Grenada, lived in Trinidad for three years, and I came to England when I was nine. If someone said to me you're going to have to retire in England, where would you live, it would be Cambridge.

I love Cambridge, it's a lovely place and I have very fond memories of my time there.

78. Coconuts

Down at an English fair
One evening I was there
When I heard a showman shouting underneath the flare

Oh! I've got a lovely bunch of coconuts
There they are all standing in a row
Big ones, small ones, some as big as your head
Give them a twist, a flick of the wrist
That's what the showman said

Oh! I've got a lovely bunch of coconuts
Every ball you throw will make me rich
There stands me wife
The idol of me life
Singing roll a bowl a ball a penny a pitch

Singing roll a bowl a ball a penny a pitch
Singing roll a bowl a ball a penny a pitch
Roll a bowl a ball, roll a bowl a ball
Singing roll a bowl a ball a penny a pitch

79. The NRE Legends

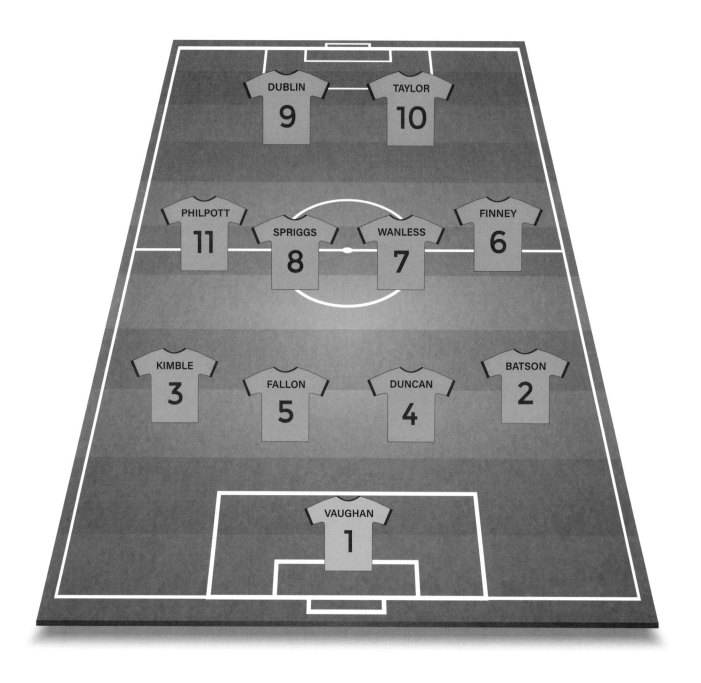

80. My Wembley goal
Dion Dublin

I scored on my debut for Manchester United, for Aston Villa, for Coventry City, and I played for England – all of that stuff is important to me, but my goal for Cambridge United against Chesterfield will always be at the top of the list. It was a dream, completely.

Many, many times I've been asked: 'What's your favourite goal? What's your best memory,' and that's my favourite memory of my whole twenty years of my career. I've played with Eric Cantona and away at Galatasaray in that incredible atmosphere, but as a personal, individual achievement, it's that goal at Wembley that takes it.

We played close to sixty games that season and that was our last one, and I like to be rewarded for hard work. I felt like we deserved it; we'd been working really hard and at the end of the season we got rewarded by going up, and I was the one who scored the winning goal.

People were talking about the long balls and all that kind of stuff, but it didn't bother me in the slightest because we were being successful. Don't be out there criticising a successful team, you can't do that, it just won't work. John Beck was right to do what he did. We played the right way at the right time and people didn't know how to handle it because it was quite new and we did it very well.

We were all on board with it and we all pulled the same way. We had about twenty, twenty-five players that said: 'Right, we're in this together. I don't care what it looks like.' We knew how to play football. There are times as a footballer when you have to do certain things to get yourself out of trouble, whether it's a flick or a turn or a dummy, you have to do them. We knew when to do them, we knew where to do them.

Whenever Becky asked us to do something, we all did it together; there were no prima donnas. That's why I think we went so far. There were people like Liam Daish, Chris Leadbitter and Tony Dennis who wouldn't accept a lack of togetherness and it rubbed off. We were all in it together.

81. Roy's boys
Roy McFarland

It wasn't about me. I had played at the highest level, represented my country, but my time at Cambridge United and that promotion team was not about me. You will not get promotion without the whole team being engaged, without them wanting to improve, and they were all brilliant – I love them, all of them.

The nice thing for me is that we all had respect for each other. When you put a shirt on for any club, whether it's Cambridge United or Manchester United, the key is to respect that shirt, respect the others who wear it and respect the people who you're representing when you put it on. Those players all did that.

I had that trio up front with Martin Butler through the middle, Trevor Benjamin on the left and John Taylor on the right. Martin would put pressure on defenders and force mistakes, Trevor had pace and power, and John had the experience.

In midfield I'd signed Ian Ashbee, who did a great job for us and went on to play at the highest level at Hull. Paul Wanless was our captain and he was just solid, he loved the game and he was the leader of that team. The maestro was Alex Russell, who had a wonderful range of passing and just a little bit of class where he could make things happen.

I had a guy there, sadly no longer with us, in David Preece who I had a great understanding with and if there were times where I made my frustrations known to the players, he would pick them up and tell them, 'The gaffer just wants you to improve, to learn.' Preecey was great for that team.

We achieved something special when we went up. To hear that the promotion under Mark Bonner was the first for Cambridge in the Football League since I was there really puts it in perspective. Crikey, it's incredible.

My time at Cambridge was a joy, I loved it. I felt I made a difference to those players. We achieved something remarkable together. I have fantastic memories of the people there and I still have great affections for the club.

82. Dave Kitson

Omer Riza

Nothing fazed Dave Kitson. He came to Cambridge from non-League as a very unassuming guy, he was very raw but with obvious quality. He used to get stick off opposition fans for his ginger hair and then he put a blonde streak in it and got even more stick, including from us – but I think that was just fuel for him. He had a hunger and aggression and you need that to succeed.

John Beck was hard on Dave but he treated him in a way that gave him the best chance to become what he ultimately became. He was tough but he always played him, giving him the opportunity to get better. He used to send Dave and Marcus Richardson round the back of the stadium to this bit of gravel with a tennis net and he would have them keeping the ball up across that, slating them whenever they got their touch wrong. Dave didn't have too much trouble with that to be fair because his touch was always good.

He had the opportunity to grow at Cambridge and we had a sort of partnership on the pitch. I could play off a big man or out wide – the two strikers I had the best parts of my career with were Ersen Martin, a Turkey international I played with at Trabzonspor, and Dave Kitson. We understood each other's games. I knew Dave could pass it with his head, and not everyone can do that, and he could get a half-turn in and pick me out in space. He knew with me that I could get beyond defenders and when I did, nobody was catching me. If I delivered for Dave, he was going to score.

I've had the pleasure of playing with great players at home and abroad. I think Dave had something as a number nine that allowed him to dominate the opposition, whether that was in the air or on the floor – he was very good technically and knew how to use his body.

He played in the Premier League and for me should have gone on to play for England. He had that quality where whatever level he played at he would have caused problems for the opposition. Maybe it didn't help Dave that he was outspoken; he knew his own mind and he wasn't afraid to speak out, but you have to respect that.

83. Away days

Andrew Leggett

I've never kept a tally of how many away games I've done, but I've been going regularly for the past twenty years so it must be at least four hundred. My dad took me to my first away game at Port Vale in the early nineties, not many kids went in those days and they had no concessions so they let me and my sister in as one adult.

There have been some huge journeys over the years, with Tuesday night games at places like Plymouth and Exeter. It often involves multiple trains or replacement bus services, with return journeys running into the early hours of the morning. There are times when Cambridge are playing badly and you wonder why you do it, but ultimately when I wake up on the morning of a match there's no way I'd want to do anything else. I do it for the love of Cambridge United.

The ideal away day for me is at a ground as far away as possible, somewhere like Barrow or Carlisle. It makes a whole day of it being on the train and meeting fans of other teams, finally arriving and hopping off at the station and knowing some people will be wondering why you've travelled all that way or maybe even have some respect for the fact you've made the effort, and of course meeting up with other Cambridge fans. To top it off you just need a United win.

My most memorable away day is actually a pre-season friendly in Germany against Wattenscheid – not many fans can say they've seen Cambridge play in Europe! It was an amazing feeling being at Stansted airport in my Cambridge shirt the day before the game knowing I was flying abroad to watch my team play.

The lockdown season was difficult because following Cambridge is a big part of my life. Luckily, we had iFollow but it's not the same as being there and I did miss that, although I was one of the lucky few who managed to get a prime spot for the Leyton Orient game. I'm glad we are all able to get to games again now and I'm looking forward to going to places like Hillsborough, The Valley, Portman Road and the Stadium of Light. There are so many great away days to look forward to.

84. Terry Eades
1944-2021

Few people attracted such universal affection as Terry Eades. Mention the name to anyone who knew him and glowing praise soon follows. He was admired on the field and adored off it.

Born in Northern Ireland in 1944, Eades began his career with Chelmsford City and moved to Cambridge United in 1968 for £2,500 – as shrewd an investment as the club have ever made. Eades went on to make 351 appearances for the U's across nine years and three divisions, proving a formidable defender no matter the level.

He was signed by legendary United manager Bill Leivers, with Eades marshalling a defence that provided the foundation for consecutive Southern League titles. It was those successes – as well as a relentless PR assault – that convinced enough Football League members to vote for United's election to the elite in 1970.

Eades himself was thrilled to see the club achieve their long-held ambition to join the League after distinguishing themselves in non-League football and he would take the step up in quality comfortably in his stride.

Indeed, David Lill felt Eades could easily have played far higher up the pyramid, having peaked at the third tier with the U's – and his sole season at that level ended in relegation. Lill paints a picture of a man whose calm and unassuming persona off the pitch masked the steely determination of a centre-half who took no prisoners when he crossed the white line. 'When he tackled someone, they stayed tackled,' said Lill. 'And when he headed the ball, he really headed it. There was nobody ever needed to pick up any pieces around him.'

Eades' farewell came as United returned to Division Three under Ron Atkinson in 1977, just as a young Steve Fallon was establishing himself. Fallon certainly felt the benefit of learning his trade alongside someone of Eades' calibre. 'He was a top man,' said Fallon, who spent twelve years with United. 'Whatever he said went. He was a wise man but he was a great bloke as well. He had this aura about him. He did everything right, he conducted himself right. What he said was gospel.'

85. The 2013-14 promotion season

UNITED BACK IN THE FOOTBALL LEAGUE

Cambridge United climbed back into the Football League after Ryan Donaldson's star performance in a 2-1 National League play-off final win over Gateshead at Wembley.

The ex-Heed player set up Liam Hughes' second-half opener before curling home a stunning free-kick, with Richard Money's men holding on after a late Jack Lester goal, despite playing with 10 men following an injury to captain Ian Miller.

United will now return to the elite 92 after spending nine years in non-League football following the club's harrowing relegation in 2005.

Donaldson, who scored twice in the FA Trophy triumph in March, claimed the Man of the Match award once again, his superb strike sparking wild celebrations on and off the pitch.

Delighted U's boss Money joined the majority of his players in celebrating a momentous campaign back at the Abbey, where fans gathered to rejoice in the club's first promotion since 1999.

It was also a dream day for Luke Chadwick and Josh Coulson, two lifelong U's fans who were able to help achieve the most important promotion in United's history.

MONEY'S EFL PRIDE

Richard Money revelled in the glory of restoring Cambridge United's status as a Football League club on a memorable day in the capital.

After a season in which the title slipped well out of his side's reach, Money expertly marshalled his charges through their play-off campaign.

Key players

Luke Berry (44 appearances, 12 goals): An all-action campaign from United's diminutive midfield dynamo, whose talent deserves to grace the Football League.

Tom Champion (46 appearances, 1 goal): The midfield anchor, ever-present and ever-reliable – the Wembley double wouldn't have been possible without him.

Ryan Donaldson (33 appearances, 5 goals): The man for the big occasion, Donaldson wowed twice on the Wembley stage to cap an impressive debut season in amber and black.

"There is a stigma about being a non-League club from people who don't really understand the level," he said. "But the fact you can now call yourself a Football League club and the players can call themselves Football League players means an incredible amount."

Pos	Team	Pld	W	D	L	GF	GA	GD	Pts
1	Luton Town	46	30	11	5	102	35	+67	101
2	Cambridge United	46	23	13	10	72	35	+37	82
3	Gateshead	46	22	13	11	72	50	+22	79
4	Grimsby Town	46	22	12	12	65	46	+19	78
5	FC Halifax Town	46	22	11	13	85	58	+27	77
6	Braintree Town	46	21	11	14	57	39	+18	74
7	Kidderminster Harriers	46	20	12	14	66	59	+7	72

86. My 100 things

Max Rushden (I misread the brief)

Tree behind the Habbin/Barrick's 25-yarder/Heathcote never being beaten/Jr U's flat cap/Bomb scare v Halifax/QUALITY/Trev at Wednesday/Forest away/Arbury Fast Fit sign/Alan Kimble's pens/Philpott's volley/Wes/Daish heading everything/Nerves when Chapple had a back pass on his left/Betting Nathan that Granville would play for England/Something Inside So Strong/ Lionel's pen/Rowett orange ball v Vale/O'Neil top left/Filan sponsored by Annabelle's Sandwich Bar/Staring at NRE from Jr U's enclosure/Leadbitter & Clayton from halfway line/Owen Nurse's voice breaking on 91 goals VHS/Raynor's looping crosses/Manuel's red cards/Vaughan/Carlo & Butts/Paul Clark assistant manager – deepest sweeper ever/Losing my voice in injury time v Gateshead/The look on Arsenal fans' faces when Dion scored/Rendell v Stevenage/Cheetham, my first fave player/Dear Devon White/Preece pinging it about/My debut in 86/Thompson's OG/ Lynfox kit/Spriggs/Howlett kit's furry inside/Hummel chevrons/Armand One/Bailie v Tranmere on waterlogged pitch/Channel balls/Clive Wilson/Wanny/Billy Beall/Norwegian at Great Barrier Reef asking if Youngs was as good as on Champ Man/Beaumont Stainless Steels stripes/Being at Orient 20-21/Craddock/Guys in NRE saying 'we never score from corners' every time we got a corner/Hitching lift for LDV final as someone recognised my voice from joke I told on terraces/ Listening on radio to Branagan saving Hoddle's pen/Di Canio's face after drawing at the Abbey/ Paul Stainton's phone-in/Dion & Beck on MOTD/First season ticket/Matt Walsham: 'I'll give you a polo every time we score' before the 5-1/Lillis' goal at London Road/Shaggy curling one past massive P*sh keeper/Lifting barrier at Comet for Fraser's car to squeeze under/Dad ringing club, getting seat next to Trevor Brooking in press box for Palace quarter-final/CUFC 0-0 Man Utd/Hyde's yellow boots/Electronic scoreboard/Allotments/Cow pats on the common/Wolfie/ Fallon/Ex-U's in the Premier League/Rumours Jason Donovan was buying us/Getting Derry the job (unconfirmed)/Taking award-winning bacon sandwich on Soccer AM/iFollow/Johnno Shouting 'Mullin'/Dion ringing me to play in a game/Falling over in said game/CUFC players in Shoot, Match or 442/Eric Clapton's Bad Love – moody theme to promotion goals videos/U's being in Sensible Soccer/Dion's England caps/Le Roy & Renard/Wembley 90/Chadwick coming home/Claridge's socks/Miller in Fez/Laurie Ryan's left foot/Tudor's barrel chest/Darler/George hoovering the Radio Cambs studio when you were on air/Chapple & Robinson v Derby/Pint in the Salisbury/We're the middle/Anglo-Italian cup/Winning at Ipswich/O'Shea/Cheers when Chapple side-footed to Fensome after Beck said we were going to pass/Going with dad/Coconuts/Hope.

87. One Wonky Antler fanzine
Owen Kiernan

In early 2001, myself and my dad Gerry decided to launch a new fanzine, as the club had been without one for a while since the demise of the Abbey Rabbit. We had a PC, an iffy copy of MS Publisher, and no small amount of enthusiasm. We announced our plans on Moosenet and the Cambridge United message board, and began to formulate something. A name was decided – One Wonky Antler, in honour of the bedraggled appearance of Marvin the Moose.

The late Andrew Bennett allowed us to reproduce his inimitable match reports, and former Rabbit editor Steve Jillings was also keen to contribute, which gave us some ready-made, high-quality content. Issue one was launched in January 2001 before the game against Notts County. We weren't permitted to sell OWA on club property. At half-time it was announced on the pitch that a new magazine was on sale outside the ground, and that it was not an official club publication and thus should not be purchased. Of course, sales rocketed after that and issue one sold out quickly after. Issue two saw an article from former Arsenal and Southend player Adrian Clarke on the effect fans can have on players and issue three saw us interview Lionel Perez.

Issue four saw some controversy, as a letter arrived at Antler HQ postmarked HM Prison Bedford. An incarcerated U's fan had written an account of his date at Peterborough Crown Court, during which he wisely decided to wear a U's shirt. Sentenced to three years, he claimed that the first year was for the burglary that had landed him there, and the next two were for wearing the shirt. The letter drew a number of complaints, including one in the official club programme, although it was a funny and well-written article, despite the strong language. Over time our relationship with the club softened, as they realised that we were selling over 500 fanzines each issue, raising a significant amount for Cambridge Fans United. Our printer, based in Cardiff, told us that we sold as many fanzines, if not more than a number of bigger clubs including some Premier League ones.

As United began to falter in the higher divisions and crowd numbers started to dwindle, we found sales were dropping – we also had a rivalry with the Planet Amber fanzine to contend with (who recycled a number of our jokes a second time!) and after a move to London I was getting to fewer games, so we handed the reins over to Ben Yelton, who carried the Antler on for two more issues before it was quietly put to bed.

88. Returning home
Liam O'Neil

I was at Cambridge as a kid when we had the likes of Trevor Benjamin and Martin Butler playing. I remember going to night games and seeing the floodlights and just being in awe of it all. When you're that age and all you want to do is play football, those are the things that you buzz about.

When Cambridge got relegated from the Football League in 2005, the Centre of Excellence was closed down and I had to leave the club I'd joined as a nine-year-old. I went to Histon but it was the Dan Ashworth connection at West Brom which got me a move up there. That's where I got my first professional contract and I'm proud to say I was able to play some games for them in the Premier League.

I was at Chesterfield when the opportunity came to move back to Cambridge, and I jumped at the chance. Even though I was dropping down a league at the time, it's a club I've always had a lot of love for and it was like returning home.

I was a little bit emotional on the last day of the promotion season; it just meant so much to me, being a Cambridge lad and a supporter growing up. It's like a boy's dream really and going up with Cambridge is the highlight of my career. We did have a wobble at the end, but to get it done on the last day made it even better. The celebrations we had all of us together, that's what football is about – we achieved something as a group, as a family.

It's weird actually because Barry Corr told me in the build-up to that game that I was going to score, and I just had a gut feeling I would. Then it actually happened – Joe Ironside got it back across goal and, I'll be honest, I just swung at it and thankfully it went in. That was just a great day and I'm proud and grateful to have been a part of it.

Football can change very quickly, but I look at Harrison Dunk and Greg Taylor and the length of service they've given the club – I'd love to do that. Those two have set the bar and they create such a good environment for everyone who comes in, and I like to think I do the same. It's been a pleasure to share a dressing room with the people I have in my time at Cambridge.

89. Reg Smart

Ste Greenall

Reg was born on the Ditton Fields estate, his father played for Cambridge and Reg was involved in the club from a young age – it was in his blood. He's sadly no longer with us but I don't think he'd object if I described him as a little bit rough and ready. However, when you got to know the man his passion for the club shone through.

He rang me up one day and said, 'I need a word with you, young man.' I'd done a bit on ClubCall about when Reg took over from David Ruston as chairman, so I thought he was going to give me a rollocking because of something I'd said in that. What he actually wanted to do was offer me the job as club secretary.

It used to be that the three most pivotal people at a club were the chairman, the manager and the secretary. Reg wasn't a great communicator and that's where I came in. I told him he needed someone who could speak to the fans and not end up arguing with them. Once I got to know Reg, I loved working with him and had the utmost respect for him.

Reg had trust in all of his managers. He was a fan so of course he had his opinions on the players and tactics and so on, but he would never tell a manager how to do his job; he let his managers manage. He had a particularly good relationship with John Beck, they were friends and they would often go out with the wives.

There was a board of six during the Beck era but it was nearly always Reg who would get the cheque book out. He would go over to Thailand every close season and leave me an open cheque, linked to his personal account, and say, 'I'd love to have that back, but if you think we need it then put down whatever number you want and take it to the bank.' That shows you the trust he had in me and the passion he had for the club.

I can sum up Reg's contribution by saying he was a very large cog in the wheel that took Cambridge United to the brink of playing in a division that no fan could have envisaged in their wildest dreams. That club beat Glenn Hoddle's Swindon, they thrashed Sheffield Wednesday, were top of the Second Division – none of that would have happened without Reg Smart.

90. Martin Butler
Trevor Benjamin

Martin was a great professional and such a good finisher. He was a good teacher as well, in terms of the way he looked after the younger lads and gave them advice, and more than anything he just showed us how to finish.

As strikers you're in competition with each other because you know the other guy is trying to take your spot, but we were different types of players and I had a lot of respect for Martin and what he could do.

It was amazing to have Martin and John Taylor to play up front with, and Michael Kyd had the benefit of that too. It was great to learn from them and add things to my game, but I was also able to be my own player and do my thing. I had the strength and the pace, I could bring other players into the game, and that added to what those guys brought to the team.

Off the pitch Martin loved a laugh and a joke so he was a great lad to have around the training ground. He was funny, very clever – and it's not that often you got that among footballers back then! He summed up what a good dressing room it was to be a part of. Roy McFarland and David Preece were great with us and we had a really good mixture of experience and youth in the team.

When Martin got his move to Reading I was happy for him, I was proud to have played a part in that and he played his part in the move that I got to Leicester. When he left I felt like I had to step up again and be the talisman for the team, because Butts had scored so many goals and obviously people were sad to see him go. After that I got to fulfil my dream of playing in the Premier League.

Martin had a great career himself and I wasn't surprised to see him do so well at Reading. He had that work rate where he was always going to make himself a success wherever he went.

We've crossed paths a couple of times since we went our separate ways and we've always had a good laugh and a reminisce about our time at Cambridge; we had some great times. I was a baby when I started at Cambridge and it's where I learned my trade, and Martin was a big part in my journey there.

91. The Lockdown Legends
Jordan Worland

It feels odd writing about the COVID pandemic when the virus still exists. But, as we emerge into something closer to normality, I keep returning to a picture of future me being asked what my abiding memory of that time is. Future me needs only two words: Lockdown Legends.

Off the pitch, as the season was halted, the club took the term 'United in Endeavour' to new levels. The Here for U's campaign pulled people together to assist the more vulnerable in society. Head coach Mark Bonner, among others, manned the phones to support those who required help with their everyday needs or just someone for company. Players donned PPE to deliver food parcels and education activity packs. The club was praised in the national press for its mental health program and its achievements supporting others. Lockdown Legends.

On the pitch, a group of unfancied players who, barring a certain former Republic of Ireland international, attracted no jealous glances from League Two's putative promotion contenders were led by a rookie manager to an achievement that exceeded even the wildest expectations of a particularly expectant wild person. Despite a rather nervy finish, the U's got across the line on the last day of the season to a secure a return to the third tier for the first time in nearly two decades.

It'll be remembered as the promotion that fans weren't actually there to see. This, however, doesn't tell the full story. With every game available to stream, the United match became a focal point of life in lockdown. Those dark months saw no socialising, no seeing family, no being in the office, and precious few opportunities to leave the house for any reason except perhaps just to say you did.

Pandemic life saw days and weeks blur into a monotonous existence – with one notable exception: 3 p.m. on Saturdays. When we really needed United to deliver, just something to distract us from the world for ninety minutes, anything to break up the gloom of living life permanently indoors, Bonner's men rose to the challenge. The squad and staff responsible for that accomplishment will forever be Lockdown Legends.

MAINSTAND D&A
www.da-rec.co.uk
D&A
D&A
www.da-training.com
D&A THE D&A MAINSTAND D&A
D&A
D&A
D&A THE D&A
MICK GEORGE GROUP
sky bet
sky bet LEAGUE TWO EFL
sky bet
LEAGUE TWO

92. 7am kick-offs
Dave Lee

It's hard to take football seriously in a country that names its top-tier teams things like 'Real Salt Lake' and 'Sporting Kansas' – producing the kind of fixtures that have me feeling very far from home, and even further from the Abbey.

Indeed, it was a big worry for me when moving to America that my chances to support the U's would become confined to Boxing Day and a handful of other opportunities. Not nearly enough to scratch that itch. If I was lucky, I thought, a fortuitous FA Cup draw might see a game sneak onto ESPN.

So when the club jumped headfirst into web streaming, I was ecstatic. My new matchday routine became a 6 a.m. alarm for a 7 a.m. kick-off – followed by either a celebratory diner breakfast or, as an Arsenal-supporting friend put it, a 'sad nap'... a return to bed that allowed you to restart your weekend, almost forgetting the events of the earlier hours had ever happened.

Of course, during the pandemic, streaming matches became the only option for most of us, no matter which side of the Atlantic we happened to live on. With normality making a slow and welcome return, international users of the iFollow service will still get to watch the 3 p.m. kick-offs back home.

For this I could not be more grateful – with me in San Francisco, my brother, Steve, in Toronto and my dad back home getting to the Abbey whenever he can, the ability to watch from afar means those lively conversations, lubricated by football, can remain as strong and meaningful as ever.

Best of all, when friends stateside ask me if I have 'adopted' a new team – as all too often they do – I can proudly say there's no need; I'm still supporting Cambridge United.

And, come to think of it, the sad naps have become far less common of late.

93. John Beck
Alan Kimble

I owe a lot to John Beck. He believed in all of us and got a group of players together and gave us a style of play that worked for us. We stuck to that style of play and it took us a long, long way.

Okay, it would have been nice for us to go that one step further and get three back-to-back promotions and be the only side to do that, but it's amazing we got so close. I owe a lot to him personally.

One thing we did have in abundance was team spirit and togetherness on and off the pitch. There was a special relationship between all the players. We all knew our jobs from day one until the day John Beck left.

My instructions were simple: two touches, out the back as quick as you can, get it in the channels as quick as you can and support your winger with the overlap. Me, Andy Fensome, Liam Daish, Phil Chapple, we all had a job: two touches, no more, that's all we could have, and then we had to stick it where it needed to go as quick as possible.

As soon as we had our second touch everyone knew where it was going: up the channel, pen them in, don't let them out and squeeze the play up. It might not have been pleasing on the eye, but that's how we got our success.

Beck had his mind games and little tricks, stuff like wanting to keep the grass long in the corners, letting the opposition team's warm-up balls down before the game and so on. We tried to do as much as we could to upset the opposition's preparation and get into their heads and thankfully that seemed to work.

He was the first person to buy into things like ice baths and we used to come in the day after games for a massage. At the end of the day, he led that football club to the pinnacle of its success and you have to give him credit for that. Yes, the players went out there and performed, but I would say it was John Beck that got us on the ladder in professional football.

94. The Abbey
Dave Stacey

I've visited my fair share of football grounds both here and abroad, well over three hundred in fact. As a groundhopper I love the buzz of walking through a turnstile and gazing upon the stands and terraces in front of me. However, there's only one place where my heart truly lies and that is, of course, Cambridge United's wonderful Abbey Stadium.

My twenty years attending the Abbey have given me things I never imagined I'd gain when sliding through the Main Stand turnstile ahead of my father as a fifteenth birthday gift. I've gained some of the best friends I could have wished for, as well as a catalogue of people I can just chat to about the U's. A football ground can also be somewhere that defines a person, can give them emotions and responses they simply don't experience in day-to-day life. In that sense, I know the Abbey has helped me to grow as a person, to mature and evolve.

I'd never felt such pain as I did at eighteen when the club dropped out of the Football League in 2005. Conversely, the happiness I felt sat in the Main Stand that first League game back against Plymouth has rarely been matched. Likewise, the pride at our monumental performance against Manchester United. I've witnessed the forging of legends such as Josh Coulson, heroes like the promotion-winning side of 2013-14 and players who have gone on to achieve at the top level.

I've been privileged to have seen games from all four stands and each provides its own unique charm. I love the sloping roof of the Newmarket Road End, the symmetry of the Habbin, the modernity of the South Stand and the views afforded by the Main Stand. The roar of a fully packed NRE can give even a hardened cynic like me chills. And at how many other grounds can you say you have to navigate through a herd of cows as you do down our east side?!

We've been told for many, many years now that to progress as a football club Cambridge United need to move away from the Abbey Stadium and into a purpose-built facility. If that should happen, they may tear down our stadium but they will never demolish our memories of a place we all call home.

95. Leyton Orient away, 2021
Thom Dobbin

The idea first occurred to me when the fixtures came out. The country was still in lockdown and a few of us were thinking of ways that it might be possible to watch a game without breaking any rules. I remembered that at Orient there were flats around the ground available on Airbnb, so I messaged the owner of one just to sound her out. She was non-committal and I didn't hear anything from her for another six months until she finally got back in touch to say she was happy to let us have the place if we stuck to the rules. She said there had been some Orient fans in the week before and the police had been called, so we were a little trepidatious.

We had a lottery to determine who was going to come out of our group of friends. Only one missed out – he had a broken wrist at the time to be fair; he took it in good grace. Our plan to be fairly inconspicuous went out of the window within about two minutes because Orient Fan TV was set up just in front of us, so we got chatting with them and I think we were picked up on iFollow as we had people messaging us asking how many of us were there (only six: me, Tom Sewell, Matt Caspell, Mark Berry, Dom Frost and Andrew Leggett).

Max Rushden was at the opposite end of the ground. We bumped into him about fifteen minutes before kick-off and we just assumed he had got in with the club somehow as we'd seen a few directors, but he told us he'd wangled himself a flat too. His story was a little different to ours as he had been approached by a guy who owned one of the flats, but that's what having a bit of a media profile does for you!

When Joe Ironside put us 1-0 up, the players ran over and celebrated with us as we were right in that corner. That was one of the defining moments of the whole night. There were a lot more twists and turns, but to be there for that moment in such a big game when we were on the brink of promotion was incredible.

Mark Bonner came over to thank us at the end, which was a really nice touch. There's a video of it but it's a little embarrassing as we'd all had a few drinks, so we may not have made much sense. But the whole experience was just amazing, and not many people can say they've had one like it. We took the biggest away following in League Two that season, that's what I like to tell everybody.

96. The 2020-21 promotion season

BONNER'S BOYS ARE GOING UP!

Mark Bonner guided Cambridge United back to the third tier for the first time in 19 years, sealing the deal with a 3-0 win over Grimsby.

The U's finally got over the line after two failed attempts to wrap up promotion, when they suffered losses to Stevenage and Harrogate.

Goals from Liam O'Neil, Wes Hoolahan and Paul Mullin saw off the Mariners to crown a memorable season played against the backdrop of a pandemic that denied fans the chance to attend the vast majority of matches.

The final-day victory on home soil ended a nervy wait to secure a top-three spot and a place in League One, with United having succumbed to a remarkable 5-4 loss at Harrogate eight days earlier.

It capped a stunning first full season in charge for Bonner, who became the first United manager to earn a Football League

promotion since Roy McFarland in 1999.

Jubilant supporters gathered in big numbers outside the Abbey to hail the achievement as the players, and indeed Bonner, appeared on the turnstile roof to celebrate with them.

BONZ ON 'ICONIC' U'S PROMOTION

Proud Cambridge boss Mark Bonner hailed his side after United's outstanding season came to a glorious conclusion.

United finished as League Two's top scorers and had the second best away record en route to claiming second spot.

But it was the wider circumstances in which the

U's achieved promotion that really struck Bonner as being exceptional.

The young United boss said: "This club will be promoted again in the future, but I'm not sure it'll be done behind closed doors, on a turnstile roof celebrating with the fans outside the stadium. It's fairly iconic."

Key players

Paul Mullin (46 appearances, 32 goals): A historic season as the striker breaks David Crown's record tally of goals in a League campaign.

Wes Hoolahan (34 appearances, 7 goals): Moments of magic too numerous to mention from 'Wessi'. An absolute joy to watch.

Kyle Knoyle (46 appearances, 2 goals): Cool, calm and collected – the full-back has everything in his game.

Pos	Team	Pld	W	D	L	GF	GA	GD	Pts
1	Cheltenham	46	24	10	12	61	39	+22	82
2	Cambridge United	46	24	8	14	73	49	+24	80
3	Bolton	46	23	10	13	59	50	+9	79
4	Morecambe	46	23	9	14	69	58	+11	78
5	Newport	46	20	13	13	57	42	+15	73
6	Forest Green	46	20	13	13	59	51	+8	73
7	Tranmere	46	20	13	13	55	50	+5	73

97. The Great Escape
Robbie Simpson

I knew how much trouble we were in when the chairman pulled me into the boot room before the Woking game and said: 'It's down to you to save Jimmy Quinn's job today!' Any doubts I had about how serious he was were removed entirely when Jez George went a step further by telling me the whole club was in danger of going under if we got relegated.

There I was, still a student at the time studying at Loughborough, and I was being tasked with saving the football club. In a weird way, I actually loved that pressure.

We had already seen Rob Newman get the sack and I was gutted for him, but with Jimmy having been a striker he was great for me. I got some real coaching on movement and the positions to take up in the box. When I managed to take all that on board it definitely made the difference; I knew where I needed to be and the goals just came much more easily.

Jimmy brought in a psychologist before the Woking game; we'd lost six in a row so we needed all the help we could get. We all had to break these wooden boards, that was part of the team talk. Darren Quinton actually couldn't break them, so I don't know what that did for his confidence! I scored twice in that game and that was the springboard for what followed.

I just went out there believing I would score every week and I ended up getting fifteen goals in the last seventeen games. The 4-0 win up at Northwich was incredible. I got my first professional hat-trick and, to this day, the second goal is in my top five – I don't think I've ever hit such a sweet strike; it just flew into the top corner.

Aldershot away is a memorable one; it was like a party atmosphere. It was a really tough, physical game and we just worked so hard, everyone was so on it and there was no way we were going to concede. With about fifteen minutes left, Courtney Pitt mishit a shot and I got on the end of it. I'm kidding, it was a genuine assist but I like to wind him up. Other than my goal against Liverpool for Oldham, I don't think I've ever felt a feeling like I did after scoring that one at Aldershot.

98. Politics and escapism
Daniel Zeichner

When I moved back to Cambridge I used to get invited to a few games by friends and it rekindled something in me. I had been a boyhood Crystal Palace supporter and regularly attended games at Selhurst Park. I lost touch with football but reconnected to it through Cambridge United.

I was working very hard to get elected in politics and didn't think I had the time for it, but I resolved to make the time. I bought a season ticket for the first season back in the Football League and absolutely loved it. I got to know people like Dave Doggett and Jez George, particularly through the Community Trust. It introduced me to the people behind the football club and I found there was so much more to it than just the game.

There are two old boys – and they won't mind me calling them that – who I sit next to in the Main Stand, Charles and Adrian, and I learn more politics from the stuff I hear on a Saturday afternoon at the Abbey than I do the rest of the week. It's part of the wider experience of going to Cambridge that I really enjoy.

There's something about being part of that crowd filtering out of the ground, down that narrow alleyway out onto Newmarket Road, that I actually find quite moving. It's an uncommon sight in modern society and there's just something about it that appeals to me.

I always say to my team to put the fixtures in my diary because, barring something dramatic, I'll be there. Weekday games are harder because sometimes you have to be in Westminster, but I get to almost all Saturday games.

As a member of parliament, you would expect me to be interested but it does come easily to me because I'm genuinely fascinated by the relationship between the club and the community. Let's be honest, the club has had its ups and downs over the years, but things have really taken on a much more positive tone and that's down to a lot of hard work from a lot of good people.

The football is of course important, but it's not just that – it's the relationships that go along with it, and I think that's what makes Cambridge such a community club.

99. Watching my son play
Paul Iredale

Jack spent his younger days playing rugby, as you do in New Zealand, but he came home one day at the age of six or seven and said, 'I want to play soccer.' Off we went down to the local school and he was unbelievable; he did things you can't coach at that age.

He kept playing when we moved to Perth and was selected for the National Training Centre under a phenomenal coach called Kenny Lowe, probably one of the best youth development coaches in the Southern Hemisphere. From there he was offered a scholarship with the Australian Institute of Sport, where he spent three years and during which time he captained Australia Under-17s when he was fifteen.

But what Jack really wanted to do was play in Europe. We have a very good friend in Perth, Steven McGarry, who played for Motherwell and St Mirren and he had contacts over in Scotland to get Jack a trial at St Mirren. That didn't work out but Greenock Morton picked him up and that's where his journey started. He made Morton's team of the decade and even played against Celtic. He was injured but came off the bench for the last ten minutes and made a couple of great runs.

I'm just a proud dad. He has a tremendous work ethic and an ability to get his head down and push through things. He was diagnosed with type 1 diabetes at thirteen and had three ACL injuries at a young age, but he just worked and worked to overcome it all.

He moved to Cambridge via Carlisle and I instantly adopted them as my club. My wife and I bought a season pass on iFollow; I'd be there in the early hours, Cambridge shirt on, coffee in hand – there was no way we'd miss a game. We have come back to the UK now and we can watch him play. I've retired so I follow Cambridge everywhere I can, I even post on the message board, although I'm sure Jack would rather I didn't.

There's a lovely vibe around the club and it's filtering down right from the top. The players have such respect for the manager and Jack is loving his time at Cambridge. Long may it continue.

100. The fans
John Taylor

I connected with the fans at Cambridge very early on. Coming from Sudbury and non-League football, I'd never experienced that support before. Having those fans on your side and playing with their backing was an unbelievable privilege for me.

There was an understanding from me that these were people who were committed to the club, who gave up their time and money to support the players who represented the club, and they understood that I was someone who wanted to do well for them. That's a connection that's lasted to this day, through good times and bad.

There are a lot of supporters who go to the Abbey now who won't have seen me play for Cambridge, but who recognise the name as being this kind of legendary figure. That comes from fans who were going long before this new generation and they pass down stories. I think that link between the old and the new is really important at a football club, and it's the supporters who create that.

These days I am one of those supporters. When I go to watch the team now, it's in that capacity as a fan, supporting those players and the manager, just as they do behind the goal at the Newmarket Road End or in the Habbin.

I'm proud to be held in the regard that I am by those fans. I remember being inducted into the club's hall of fame and how emotional I was about that. It's an amazing honour. I've been through some tough times in my life but I've always been made to feel valued by Cambridge fans.

There are people who have Cambridge United running through their blood and I'm definitely one of those. If Cambridge United ask me to do something, I will do it to the best of my ability, come what may. Paul Wanless is another of those in that category, and Josh Coulson is another one. We are the people who understand Cambridge and who want to give a little back to the football club and the fans who gave us so much.